What Others are Saying
about *Unexpected Kindness*

Unexpected Kindness is about much more than kindness. The stories Dr. Vitale shares demonstrate that through openness, curiosity, the willingness to listen, learn, and implement expert advice, you can create an abundant and fulfilling life, and lifelong friends. When you look for kindness, you'll always find it . . . even if it starts by reviewing the past, it will give you another chance to recognize and appreciate people who came into your life. He has shown us a great exercise that we all can do, so we too can recognize, appreciate, and re-energize our life through the lens of kindness. A must-read for anyone who desires to reignite their life and work, and create more kindness in this world.

—Rosie Aiello, CEO and Founder
www.TheLoveisKindNetwork.com

When was the last time you took time to recognize the acts of kindness in your life that you have been blessed with? In *Unexpected Kindness*, Dr. Joe Vitale shares some of his life changing acts of kindness that influenced him for the better, while allowing the reader to get to know him on a personal level. This will lift you up and have you reflect on your own life and how you have been blessed by others. This book is like *Chicken Soup for the Soul*.

—Mathew Foster, The Success Mentor

T0037843

This book has the potential of being the greatest book ever to mankind. This book will unlock unexpected kindness in the world. The world needs this book now to show us the way to be more kind in order to receive kindness.

—Frank Natie

Unexpected Kindness is an incredible treasure trove, a lovely collection of gems from Joe Vitale as he recalls the gifts of kindness that people have given him over the years. The stories are amazing, humorous, touching, and inspiring, reminding us of the heartwarming kindness that people show each other, and giving us the opportunity to consider how we may practice more unexpected kindness in our world where it is so needed. The book is an absolute joy to read!

—Ron Rowe, systems specialist, educator, and visionary for personal and global wellbeing

This book is a lantern. Joe not only brings light to many unexpected kindnesses he's experienced in his life, but with his stories he offers you kindnesses you don't expect.

—Rob White, Author, *The Maestro Monologue*

If you, like me, are a fan of Dr. Joe's work and books, you are in for a treat. In this book, you will get a peek into a very different lifestyle of Dr. Joe. I love how vulnerably he shares about his struggle years when fame and fortune seemed distant like a dream. I was fascinated reading how even as a kid he had so much passion and such a vast range of interests! Most importantly the stories of random acts of kindness shown to him during his struggle years will give you hope, warm your heart, and revive your faith in humanity. You will be reminded how simple it is to brighten someone's else's day by showing unexpected kindness. I can already think of what kinds of things I can do for others regularly. I know you will too!

—Shalini Joshi Yamdagni, International pain relief expert, author, *Instant Pain Relief*

Also by Dr. Joe Vitale

Faith

Expect Miracles

Zero Limits

The Miracle

The Art and Science of Results

The Fifth Phrase

The Abundance Paradigm

Karmic Marketing

The Secret to Attracting Money

Your Unlimited Self

UNEXPECTED
KINDNESS

*Autobiographical
Stories of Gratitude*

DR. JOE VITALE

MEDIA

MEDIA

Published 2024 by Gildan Media LLC
aka G&D Media
www.GandDmedia.com

Front cover design by David Rheinhardt of Pyrographx

Interior design by Meghan Day Healey of Story Horse, LLC

Library of Congress Cataloging-in-Publication Data is available upon request

ISBN: 978-1-7225-0669-8

10   9   8   7   6   5   4   3   2   1

Dedicated to the late great Bob Proctor

"Kindness is invincible."

—MARCUS AURELIUS

Foreword

Along the pathway of life, elements of beauty and magic appear that change our lives. The four-leaf clovers, radiant and unexpected rainbows, shooting stars, falling in love, holding a puppy, or maybe the first time you ride a bike, give that feeling of letting go. Those moments that free us, that glee us, that open us to be more, become more.

I had one of the moments the first time I met Dr. Joe Vitale. I first met his smile, his radiant energy, and his rambunctious light. His effervescent presence and his wide, open heart. I felt in that moment that I had met destiny, met kindness, met compassion, met care, met genius, met wisdom, and met my inner child all at once.

I felt like the world opened and that anything was possible. True rich conversations, unlimited dreams, infinite possibilities, and so much space. Yes, space like a field, a mountain range, or a sea that seems to go on forever.

I remember when my niece and nephew were small, I took them to a place called Wannado City. It was a smorgasbord of possibilities and play. Here you could Want to Do anything. You could be a firefighter, or a judge, a beautician, or own a store, you could be a doctor, or a florist, anything you wanted to do, you could imagine, dream, step into, and become. Here in front of me was a man who personified the Wannado—all in his being. "What do you want to do?" his soul seemed to ask. Not just to me but to everyone he would meet. He was the dream maker and the dream weaver.

I have spent my life touching hearts and keeping the essence of wonder and kindness alive on the planet. It has been my path without any second thought. Kindness is my nature, my essence, my being, and my way of life. I have been noted as the Ambassador of Kindness around the world. I am sent into global situations where they believe communication is not possible and I say hello. I would hope that when people meet me, they don't see a woman, or my nationality, or my hair color, or the color of my skin, my lips, or my eyes, but that they see love, kindness, compassion, care, oneness, unity, peace, and hopefully humor, laughter, joy, and the spark of life. I don't want to bring love. I want to be love itself.

Every step of the way I have thought of Dr. Joe Vitale and his magical and marvelous way of touching the world. Several years ago, we were attending a Transformational Conference and Joe surprised us all with his music. His music was a new skill that he had now mastered, and I was quite literally blown away. Yes indeed, the Want a Do

City existed inside this man. Anything he wanted to do, he mastered and shared with the world. Amazing. Inspirational. Phenomenal. And a gift to life itself.

My companies are Artistry in Motion and Unlimited Life. At age eleven, I took my first trapeze class, and the catcher told me, "Don't look for me, don't reach for me. I am the catcher; I will catch you. It is your job to swing and let go." My job has been to swing and let go in life. Now, here is a man who not only creates every dream into manifestation, but he shares with the world the secret of how to get there by teaching *Zero Limits*, based on his bestselling book: the true way and essence we can all live our lives.

It's the first ride on the bike, that glee and that freedom that you feel. Dr. Joe Vitale along the way created a masterpiece of work on PT Barnum, being a flyer through life. This has soared my soul to heights unimaginable and beyond written words.

Now comes the cherry on the sundae. The tour de force of love. Dr. Joe Vitale has shown us once again his roadmap to success. His blueprint for unlimited living, zero limits, and love. He has "unfurled" the treasure map and opened it up for all to see. He has shared the pathway to the gold inside each of our lives and into each of our hearts. He has opened the door to the secret of life.

Dr. Joe Vitale's book on *Unexpected Kindness* shows us how every moment of our life can be a defining moment that changes our lives. Dr. Joe Vitale shows us how simple acts of kindness and care changed his world, elevated his life, directed his path, and opened the view, showing the way, and infinite possibilities of success, abundance, happiness, zero limits, and a life filled with joy, exuberance, and happiness.

What do you Want to Do?

Imagine a roadmap to happiness in one book of kindness, an unexpected gift to your heart, and the gold in us all. That is this book.

Read it and, as Joe likes to say, "Expect Miracles."

—Dame Nicole Brandon
Ambassador of Kindness

"So many gods, so many creeds,
So many paths that wind and wind.
While just the art of being kind,
Is all the sad world needs."

—ELLA WHEELER WILCOX

Acknowledgments

"A kind word never broke anyone's mouth."
—IRISH PROVERB

Many helped me polish this little book. Mathew Foster, Frank Natie, Ron Rowe, Rob White, and Shalini Joshi Yamdagni, all members of a private Master Mind Alliance I ran in 2022, were early readers who gave excellent feedback. Lisa Winston, my love, was the first to read the earliest draft and offer input. I'm forever grateful for everyone in my Miracles Coaching program for their ongoing support and continual acts of unexpected kindness. Chuck Pennington created the book's website at www.UnexpectedKindnessBook.com.

Introduction

In a world that often seems fueled by conflict, disagreement, and strife, it is more crucial than ever to recognize the transformative power of kindness and compassion. *Unexpected Kindness* is a testament to the capacity of these qualities to bring about profound change, both on an individual level and within society as a whole.

As we navigate the challenges of the twenty-first century, we are confronted with an ever-expanding array of divisive forces. Social media, politics, and the breakneck pace of modern life can easily leave us feeling disconnected, disheartened, and even hostile toward one another. Yet, the antidote to these maladies lies within our grasp, embedded in the very essence of what makes us human—our innate ability to express and receive kindness.

Unexpected Kindness invites you to explore the many facets of these qualities, from the smallest gestures to the grandest acts. The stories within these pages will take you on a journey, revealing how even the simplest of kind actions can resonate deeply and reshape our world.

Ultimately, *Unexpected Kindness* serves as a reminder that compassion transcends borders, backgrounds, and beliefs, uniting us in our shared humanity. By exploring the untapped potential of kindness, we can reclaim our connections to one another and rediscover the boundless strength that lies within our collective spirit.

Unexpected Kindness will inspire you to embrace and celebrate the kindness in your life, to share it freely with others, and to become an agent of positive change in a world that desperately needs it. As you turn these pages, may you be reminded of the healing power of empathy and the extraordinary potential for transformation that resides within each and every one of us.

Expect Miracles.

Joe Vitale

> *"Tenderness and kindness are not signs of weakness and despair, but manifestations of strength and resolution."*
>
> —KAHLIL GIBRAN

When I was barely a teenager in the mid-1960s, I day-dreamed about the various roles I could play in life:

Boxing champion

Famous magician

Preacher

Attorney

Author Hypnotist

FBI agent

In nearly each case, I reached out to someone noteworthy in the field—if not legendary—and asked for help. I never thought much of it, or how daring it was for me to write living legends and expect a reply, but their replies were glorious acts of unforgettable and unexpected kindness.

Especially to a kid.

The only person who didn't write back to me was Groucho Marx. Considering he was elderly and known for his belligerent gruffness, it was probably an act of unexpected kindness that he didn't. He may have crushed me.

I wanted to be heavyweight boxing champion of the world. I idolized the greats. I watched old films of them boxing. I read biographies. I watched mainstream pugilistic movies, like Errol Flynn playing James J. Corbett in *Gentleman Jim*. I thought I could be one of those boxing greats.

How hard could it be?

That was long before I met actual champions Floyd Patterson, George Foreman, and Mike Tyson. Seeing them when I was an adult made me realize those giants would have turned me to dust with a look. But my teenage mind dreamed of winning.

Jack Dempsey had been one of the greatest early boxing champions. He was still alive in 1970, so I wrote to him. He sent back an autographed photo of himself in his prime. I still have it. I loved his humbleness as well as his style. He signed it "Love," which seemed odd for a man known to knock people unconscious.

After reading a biography of Houdini, and seeing the famous Tony Curtis movie about the magician, I wanted to be the next world-famous escape artist.

But Houdini was long dead so I couldn't learn from him. I did try reaching him through a séance, though.

I still remember my father asking, "What's a séance?" and his very confused face as he tried to process my answer ("It's a way to communicate with the spirit world, Dad."). Anyway, Houdini has not been able to escape death yet. No reply.

John Mulholland was a famous magician, author, and editor. He knew Houdini's wife. I wrote to him asking for advice about being a professional magician.

He wrote back a two-page typewritten letter. He detailed what I would need to know and the challenges that lay ahead. His letter became famous and was later published in *Magic* magazine. I still have it.

As I read about parapsychology and the supernatural, in a search for real magic, I reached out to authors who stood out as experts.

Hans Holzer was a prolific writer in the field of the unusual. I had visited a haunted house in Pennsylvania and wrote to Holzer to ask if it were the real deal.

He was kind and wrote back, scribbling on my letter, "Probably a fake."

I was looking for life answers as a kid. My father remembers me trying to add a chapter to the Bible. My parents thought I might be a preacher or priest.

Billy Graham was a famous evangelist. He had charisma and oratory skills. He hung out with celebrities. He went on talk shows. He held crowds and saved crowds.

I wrote to him, telling him I was thinking of being a preacher. He wrote back, but today I can't find the letter. I don't recall it being personal or persuasive, but I do remember it was an act of unexpected kindness from a legend in his field.

Clarence Darrow was a famous trial lawyer. He was probably most famous for the controversial Scopes Monkey Trial and the Leopold and Loeb murder case. I had seen a movie, *Compulsion*, about one of his cases, with Orson Welles playing Darrow.

I was fascinated by Darrow's charisma, oratory, and persuasion skills. I went to the library and read books about him. Darrow died in 1938, but he had been born and raised in Kinsman, Ohio, which wasn't far away from my hometown of Niles.

I got in the car and drove to his birthplace. Nothing there kept my inspiration going but I remember the unexpected kindness of the man living where Darrow was born. He showed me around. Chairs were being made there with Darrow's name on them. The man answered my questions. I never forgot his heart.

E.B. White was famous for his children's books. But I loved his how-to book, *The Elements of Style*.

I wrote to him, asking for advice on being a writer. He sent back a run-on sentence typed on a single sheet of paper. I found the line almost incomprehensible. I thought White needed an editor for his private correspondence. I don't know what happened to the letter.

Rod Serling was the man behind most of the famous *Twilight Zone* TV episodes. I marveled at his writing skill. When he came to Youngstown, Ohio, around 1970, I went to meet him.

I nervously asked if he planned to write an autobiography. He was kind and way too humble.

"Nothing interesting has happened to me," he said, shrugging off the idea.

I decided right then to become an author. If he could be so insecure and yet so successful, then I had a chance too. Serling's biographers have found treasure in his life, but Serling didn't see it. I related to his low self- esteem. It gave me hope.

When I considered being a hypnotist, I reached out to Sidney Petrie, who had a practice in New York City. He founded The Institute for Hypnotherapy in 1957. He had coauthored several popular books on hypnotism and self-hypnosis with Robert Stone. I wrote Petrie a letter.

He had passed away by then, so I later learned, but his son replied. I bought a few reel-to-reel hypnosis tapes and practiced them. I loved and still love hypnosis. It's obvious from my books, such as *Hypnotic Writing*, and from the fact that I named my company, Hypnotic Marketing, Inc.

When I considered being an FBI agent, I wrote to the man in charge: J. Edgar Hoover.

He wrote or dictated a letter to me. He explained I would need a law degree and, as I remember, law enforcement experience. After that, I could apply with the FBI. To my teenage mind, it seemed like more than I could handle.

But I did study with a police chief in my small town. My father knew him. He taught me fingerprinting: how to take them and read them. I was the first Boy Scout in the history of scouting to be awarded a fingerprinting merit badge. That policeman was truly unexpectedly kind to me.

And I still know how to read fingerprints.

None of these legends had to respond. I was a kid. A nobody. They were clearly celebrities. But they each took time to show unexpected kindness. It has never been forgotten.

Today, I try to help anyone who contacts me with a sincere plea or question. I'm trying to practice unexpected kindness, too. How about you?

> *"'Nothing,' wrote Tolstoy, 'can make our life,
> or the lives of other people, more beautiful
> than perpetual kindness.'"*
> —GRETCHEN RUBIN

The librarian in my junior high school, Mrs. Pruitt, was a short, plump, big-smiling, outgoing lady who liked to talk, support kids, and do events.

I liked her.

She liked me.

She encouraged me to be on the yearbook committee, write for the school newspaper, and even work in the library.

Considering how withdrawn, introverted, self-conscious, immature, and insecure I was, it's a miracle she warmed me out of my shell at all.

Somehow, she arranged for me to give a speech to the school before an assembly meeting.

I have no idea why I agreed. I was terrified of people and of speaking anywhere, to anyone, except immediate family and a handful of close friends.

Speak on stage? Me? To the whole school? What was I thinking?

Mrs. Pruitt wanted me to lead people in the Pledge of Allegiance before the meeting. But she wanted me to explain the pledge, and then encourage people to really feel what they were saying when they repeated the pledge.

I remember her assuring me I could do it. I wrote out my speech and showed it to her. She made a few suggestions but basically left it as is. Her lack of criticism helped me believe in my words and myself.

On the day of the event, I had my suit jacket from the Goodwill, and a snap on fake tie, as I didn't know how to tie a real one. I stood backstage, waiting.

A smart-aleck kid walked up and tore off my fake tie.

Then, as now, I'm stunned and speechless when someone does something rude and ridiculous. I just can't comprehend their reasoning.

Fortunately, the child gave me back my tie and I was able to snap it back on.

I kept reviewing my paper. Mrs. Pruitt asked how I was.

"I have a problem," I told her, stammering.

"Yes?"

"I don't actually know the pledge of alliance."

I was embarrassed to admit it. Everyone assumes because school always began with the pledge, that we all had it memorized. Not me. I just mumbled sounds that were close to the words I heard as kids in classrooms said the actual words.

"You don't know it?"

"Not by heart. I memorized my speech but not the pledge."

It was ironic that my speech was about the importance of the pledge, and yet there I was, without the pledge in my memory.

"Everyone else knows it," she said. "You just start it and follow the crowd."

Ironically, that's what I had been doing every day. I took a big breath and got on stage.

People stared.

They hung on my words.

I had a sense that I had some sort of command for those brief moments.

I started the pledge and sure enough, everyone said it. I did my best to follow along but truthfully it felt like they were waiting on me.

"You did great," Mrs. Pruitt said afterwards. "I'm proud of you."

Her encouragement, her push, her belief, and her friendship stayed with me for decades. When she retired and moved to Florida, and I escaped Ohio for my hell years in Houston (more on that later), she wrote me an occasional letter.

I have never forgotten her unexpected kindness. I've often said that you can accomplish much if you have someone who believes in you almost more than you believe in yourself.

Mrs. Pruitt believed in me.

> *"For attractive lips, speak words of kindness."*
> —AUDREY HEPBURN

Probably thanks to David Carradine and the TV series, Kung Fu, I wanted to learn karate. I was already into boxing. My father supported any form of fitness or self-defense, so he quickly and eagerly agreed to sign me up for a karate class, circa 1969.

I loved it.

It was taught by A. E. Vea, an eccentric entrepreneur with a black belt and a beer belly.

I never forgot how Mr. Vea handled my father at the demo for the class.

Mr. Vea was demonstrating kicks and blocks, stopping attackers, and more. He would ask for volunteers from the audience. I was one of them. Vea brought his foot up to an inch from my chin. A photographer took the shot. It ended up in the local newspaper the next day.

Ah, a taste of fame.

My brothers and I urged my father to get up there when Vea asked for volunteers. We knew he was a boxer. We knew he was a Marine. We knew he was tough.

But my dad hushed us.

After the demo, my dad went up to the instructor.

"Mr. Vea, my kids wanted me to step up when you asked for volunteers," my dad said, as we boys stood by. "But I'm a professional fighter trained to hit and kill. I can't pull my punches. If you and I got into it, there'd be blood."

Mr. Vea was the coolest man I had ever seen. He radiated charm like the sun shining on grapes.

He put his hand on my dad's shoulder and said, "I didn't want you to come up. I wanted some smart ass that I could put in their place. If you came up, you'd hit me and make me look bad."

My dad laughed.

Even as a kid I knew it was smooth. He made my dad look good in front of his kids. He saved my dad's honor.

A year or so later, I went to Mr. Vea because he was training a female black belt champion. I was a writer. I wanted the story.

Mr. Vea agreed. He took me to lunch at an Italian deli. Turns out he owned it. He was probably the first entrepreneur I ever met. He let me interview the black belt and write the story. I admired him, but he was an enigma. Even his name, he said, wasn't his real one.

He influenced my life, and I would circle back and see him again about fifty years later . . .

As I learned karate and read about martial arts, I discovered Aikido. Aikido seemed more loving, gentle, easy, and doable. But I couldn't find an Aikido instructor. So I sent a letter to Black Belt magazine, saying I was a teenager needing an Aikido instructor to teach me. The magazine, acting from unexpected kindness, ran the letter.

I got calls and letters from around the world. Most of the people wanted large sums of money to travel to the US and teach me. My father turned them all away, even refusing long distance collect calls from places like Guam.

By the time I got to college, still in need of an instructor, one man with a black belt in Aikido who lived an hour away said he'd come and teach classes if I got a group together.

I awkwardly went to the college activities committee, found out how to get a room, and booked it. Then I wrote the first ad of my life, a flyer for a free intro to Aikido, and I posted it everywhere.

It turns out my first Aikido promotion worked.

About thirty people showed up. The instructor showed up, gave his demo, and about half of the people registered for classes. The first ever Kent State University Aikido Club was born, circa 1972. Despite my lack of confidence in myself, I pulled it off. And everyone was kind.

Fast forward fifty years.

In 2019, I wanted to remember some of the things I learned in the first karate class, from around 1970. There was a swinging two-arm movement that made me virtually invincible. But I couldn't remember all of it. Five decades had passed.

I researched, looked in books, asked around. Nothing.

Then I wondered if the original instructor was still around. He'd be elderly but maybe he'd remember me. I looked online. Nothing. But I was planning a trip back home to Ohio to see my family, so I could ask around then.

I learned that Mr. Vea was alive. He had had a heart attack and a stroke, and dementia was setting in, but he clearly remembered me.

We had lunch together.

"I remember you well," he said. "You had two brothers and a sister who all attended my YMCA classes."

I was impressed.

I told him about the movements I was trying to remember. He said he'd teach me.

We went back to his school—he still had the space, but others taught in it—and he showed me the maneuvers. It was clear he didn't quite remember it all, but he was kind and patient with me.

At the end, he presented me with a patch of progress. I've never forgotten the unexpected kindness.

> *"Kindness is the only service that will stand the storm of life and not wash out. It will wear well and will be remembered long after the prism of politeness or the complexion of courtesy has faded away."*
>
> —ABRAHAM LINCOLN

One of the notable thinkers I reached out to early on was Win Wenger. But he wasn't just a thinker. He was a genius.

My intense reading of books from the library caused me to stumble across true gems. He wrote *How to Increase Your Intelligence* in 1975. Wenger was an author teaching people how to think. He focused on creativity. His mind was busy, prolific, dynamic, unrestricted, and joyful.

I called him.

I was a high school student (or maybe in college at Kent State University by then) and he was a blossoming author slowly getting attention for his inventions and solutions. He was unexpectedly kind to me. We stayed in contact by mail. I bought all his books, booklets, and special reports.

Even as my life took sharp lefts and bottomed out at times, Win was there, always available. When I landed in Texas circa 1978 and was struggling to make a name for myself in the 1990s, I called him.

"How'd you get in Texas?" he asked.

I was shocked that he even remembered me at all.

He followed my career. As I got better known for my marketing skills, he told people about me. He was the man who introduced me to Mark Joyner, who later became another significant player in my life.

I quoted Win's methods in my book on P.T. Barnum in 1998, and in my first audio program for Nightingale-Conant in 1999.

As the wheels of karma turned, I was able to return some favors to him and others. Once I was in the good graces of Nightingale-Conant with my first audio program, I told them about Win. By then he had coauthored a book called *The Einstein Factor*. Due to my introduction, Win's program was recorded. It felt great to return some unexpected kindness to him.

> *"My wish for you is that you continue.*
> *Continue to be who and how you are, to astonish*
> *a mean world with your acts of kindness.*
> *Continue to allow humor to lighten*
> *the burden of your tender heart."*
>
> —MAYA ANGELOU

Around 1978, I was out of homelessness but barely on the upper limit of poverty.

I was in Houston.

I was broke.

Struggling.

Desperate.

Because I wasn't afraid of hard work or intense labor, due to what felt like a lifetime on the railroad tracks as a gandy dancer (laborer), I got a job with an industrial cleaning company.

I didn't know what I was in for, however.

I was on a crew that went inside oil tanks in the humongous refineries of Deer Park, outside of Houston. I still wasn't accustomed to the heat and humidity of Texas. Add in dressing up in protective suits and wearing goggles, and going inside enclosed metal tanks, carrying, and using high pressure water hoses, and it's a recipe for near death.

It was all dangerous.

The chemicals in the tanks were lethal. The chemicals we used to clean the tanks were lethal. And all of it was explosive.

In fact, the crew I began with, months after I left, all died when a chemical fire broke out. The entire group burned to death.

But before I left that company, I befriended one fellow who seemed more levelheaded and relatable to me.

Ken was polite, professional, friendly, walked with bowlegs and a limp, and was a little older than me. He took an interest in my life and struggles. He listened as I painted a life of being an author. He was supportive.

He also helped me when I bought a $300 Volkswagen Beetle that wouldn't run. He often drove to my dump of a place, stayed under the car with me all night, and worked until the car was running.

One night, after a particular struggle to get the car fixed, it finally turned on. He put his arm on my shoulder. Our eyes met. We smiled. It was a symbol of celebration.

We won.

When I married my first wife in 1979, we went to Ken's for dinner. He had a wife and son. His wife worked running a security guard agency. She had given a talk at a dinner the week before and had the cassette recording of it. But he didn't have a player.

Ken dropped everything and went to the store to buy a cassette player. It cost $30. I was broke, so his spending thirty dollars became inspiring to me.

I told my wife, "I want to be able to go to the store and buy anything I want."

Besides all this kindness, Ken one day fried me with a gift I couldn't thank him enough for.

He drove a two-door hot rod that he loved. It wasn't anything like a race car and it wasn't expensive, but for a working stiff, it was cool.

He knew I loved the car. He knew I needed a reliable car. So, one day, he gave it to me.

"You can have it," he said.

I stuttered but couldn't speak.

"Just take over the payments," he said. "No credit check. No deposit needed. No forms to fill out. I'll hand you the payment book. That's it."

I choke up even now, decades later, remembering this moment. "Just don't miss any payments," Ken said, smiling. "Or they'll come after me."

The payments were doable, especially compared to the kind of payments I make for my Bentley today. I accepted Ken's gift, took the payment book, and honored his request: I made payments every month.

And I loved that car.

It's now been decades and I though can't remember the make or model of the car, I do remember Ken and his unexpected kindness.

> *"Your acts of kindness are iridescent wings*
> *of divine love, which linger and continue to*
> *uplift others long after your sharing."*
> —RUMI

Bruno Reich wasn't a nice man.

He was tall, loud, opinionated, and rough. He was the son of my landlord when I lived in a dump in Houston for twelve years. I could barely afford the cheap room. Life was a struggle. When the landlady died, Bruno took over. He could have evicted me, and I feared he might, but he maintained the home and let me stay there. It was an uncharacteristically nice thing to do. He talked about selling it to me, but I was in no position to buy any house.

Bruno didn't believe in self-help or positive thinking. I told him I was reading Norman Vincent Peale's book on the power of positive thinking. He said, "You believe that shit?"

"Yes!" I defensively said. "It works." "It's working for you?"

"I'm counting on it."

He didn't press me, but it was clear he thought I was nuts. But he noticed I played the harmonica.

"How long you been playing?" he asked. "Maybe a year."

"Have you ever tried the guitar?"

"I wanted to play as a kid, but my dad bought me an accordion. He wanted to hear polkas."

"You only need three chords, and you can sing songs," he said. I didn't know why he was telling me.

"I would go to parties with a guitar, and everyone would look at me," he went on. "You ought to play since you already enjoy the harmonica."

I nodded, not sure what to say.

Bruno came out and handed me a guitar. "Try this."

I held it but didn't know what to do. "I've had this thing for decades," he said.

"Looks cool," I mumbled, not knowing why I was even holding it.

"You can have it."

What?

I felt the guitar. It was real. Wood. And heavy. "You're giving this to me?"

"Yes, if you think you'll play it."

"I'd love to play it."

"All I ask is you never sell it. Give it away one day if you want but don't ever sell it."

It was an old Harmony, probably from the old Sears catalog of the 1950s. It had a thick baseball bat neck. It was dark wood, heavy, and probably built to take a beating, whether heavy strumming or using it as a weapon. I didn't know how awkward it was to play because I didn't have anything to compare it to.

I took a few guitar lessons with that guitar. That's when I learned the neck was almost too thick for my hand to grip. Still, it was a guitar. And Bruno gave it to me.

Years later I saw him, and he asked if I had the guitar.

"I do and I'm still grateful."

"How many chords do you know?"

"About thirty."

He was speechless.

"You only need three," he said.

More years passed and my name was out there as a successful published author, yet before *The Secret* came out. Bruno wrote me an email.

"Is it true?"

"Is what true?"

"You seem successful. Congrats, if it's true."

He was still thinking of me as the broke and awkward guy who could barely pay rent for an empty room yet had dreams of being a published author. I have no idea if he saw my rise to global fame after *The Secret* came out and I appeared on Larry King. Bruno had had a heart attack early on. Seeing me on Larry King probably would have stopped his heart entirely.

I still have the guitar he gave me. While I've sold a lot of guitars over the years, I've never even considered selling that one. Whenever I look at it, I remember Bruno's good deed, and I wonder who will receive it next.

> *"I was in darkness, but I took three steps and found myself in paradise. The first step was a good thought, the second, a good word; and the third, a good deed."*
>
> —FRIEDRICH NIETZSCHE

My first wife and I got up at five o'clock every Saturday morning and drove to the laundromat. We did this weekly for twelve years.

We didn't have the money to buy a washer and dryer. We didn't have room for it while we lived in the one-bedroom efficiency. So, we made the laundromat excursion weekly. We always went early to avoid crowds and be sure we had washers and dryers to use. Getting the coins together was always a challenge, and that usually made me feel poor.

The couple that opened the laundromat and ran it got to know us. Mr. Bean was a true old-world Texan. He talked slow, barely moved his lips, had squints for eyes, and walked with steel beam back pride. He was funny in a southern way, making statements that were understatements.

His wife was shy, hardworking, loyal, and religious. When one of her kidneys gave out, she went on weekly dialysis. I don't remember if it lasted months or years. But one day Mr. Bean announced, "She healed it."

"What?"

"She's healed," he said. "She prayed and got a miracle."

It was one of the first stories I heard from an actual person that prayer worked. Decades later, I would write an entire book about it (*The Secret Prayer*), but back then, it was a stunning thing to hear.

They grew to like us. We grew to know them. They were already elderly but worked hard. When my wife and I finally got a place to live, Mr. Bean offered to buy us a washing machine. He did too. He and his wife came and saw that it was delivered to us.

We would never see him again, and everyone at the laundromat knew it, given he and his wife were so elderly and we were moving far away with our laundry equipment, but we never forgot his unexpected kindness, especially on laundry day.

> *"Never lose a chance of saying a kind word."*
> —WILLIAM MAKEPEACE THACKERAY

Everyone suffers at some point in their lives, but my first wife and I had a miserable time for more than ten years after we were married in Houston in 1979.

I was living in a dump. It was one room in a house. The room had a toilet, a TV, and a sofa bed all in the same room.

Why my wife left her job and apartment in Oregon to move in with me is a testament to her love.

I sure had nothing to offer.

We stayed in the room for over a decade. I always felt trapped.

The landlady liked me and as she grew older, and I helped her maintain the property and the rental units she had in the back, she gave me an additional room in the house. It helped but was certainly not luxurious, or comfortable, or private.

Still, we stayed.

I couldn't see a way out.

My wife became an alcoholic there. She came out of the other room one night and said, "I have a problem."

I was stunned. I was frozen.

"I have been drinking and hiding it," she confessed.

She showed me bottles under the sink. She showed me bottles hidden in the trash can.

I felt stupid to be so oblivious to her drinking. I felt confused to how she afforded it. And she's looking at me, trusting I can save her from herself. But I didn't know what to do.

I called a doctor through the health insurance she had from work, and he said, "Take her to the emergency room right now."

I did. They took her and kept her. For the next week, she detoxed.

For the next eighteen years, she went to Alcoholics Anonymous (AA).

I always admired her strength in asking for help, and in maintaining sobriety. I wish I could have given her more. But thanks to the unexpected kindness of a stranger, we both got something big and life changing.

Let me tell you the story . . .

Our little room was an embarrassment. I could never bring anyone over.

I didn't want to act successful but live as a failure. I was trying to get published.

I started teaching adult education classes and made some money, but not enough to escape.

And I didn't have faith in my ability to pay for a house or an apartment or anything else.

We struggled. We hurt.

I was working for an oil company on the other side of town during some of this time. Most lunches were taken at the food court at the local mall. But one day my gut told me not to go there. It suggested I turn left.

To my surprise, I discovered an Italian deli nearby.

I went in, ordered, and ate a sandwich that brought back a flood of memories of home and family and lost love. I told the owner how pleased I was. He thanked me but didn't seem to sense my true gratitude.

Back in my office, I used the company equipment to make a new menu for the deli.

I made copies of the menu and gave them to the owner. I also told everyone at the oil company about him.

Suddenly the little deli was getting regular business. And lots of it.

To thank me, he gave me free lunch for the next year. It was unexpected kindness but nothing like what he was about to do for me.

There was no way to prepare for it or believe it.

My parents flew down to visit us. It was embarrassing because we didn't have anywhere for them to stay. I asked a kind neighbor to put them up. They agreed.

The deli owner offered to make a special dinner for my parents.

He did. It was time-consuming and delicious beyond belief. He made it an occasion with tablecloths on a day he normally was closed.

He fed my wife and I, and my parents, and my cousin from Corpus Christi. And he only charged one hundred dollars—enough to cover his costs.

But as unexpectedly kind as that was, it wasn't the biggest gift he gave us.

Over lunches throughout the next year, I would complain about where I lived, the long commute to get to and from work, how miserable my life was as I struggled to be an author, and how embarrassed I was to live in the rooms.

The little man from Italy listened. He had no words of comfort or wisdom. But often all we need is to be heard.

He heard me.

And then one day he said he was going to sell his home. He built the house for his family decades earlier. He planted fig trees from Italy. He decorated it with figurines and mementos from Italy. He said the house had been empty for over a year because he was too attached to it to sell it. His family had already moved into another home. He didn't have his old home on the market yet.

He asked me if I wanted to see it.

I did. I loved it. So, I brought my wife out to see it, and she loved it.

Compared to the basic rooms we had been in, a three-bedroom brick home, complete with garage, fireplace, and a yard seemed ideal.

There was just one problem. I had no credit.

While I worked for the oil company, I had dependable income. But I wanted to be an author. I didn't plan to stay employed. So how could I buy a house?

"I'll owner finance," Mike said. "You just make payments to me."

It's hard to imagine the relief this unexpected gift brought my wife and me. It was a turning point. It was a sharp pivot in our life path. Finally having our own home gave us both a feeling of security, self-worth, and hope.

I have never forgotten Mike or his unexpected kindness.

Years later, when my first wife died, Mike came to the funeral. I hadn't seen him in years at that point, but his thoughtfulness touched me.

How do I say thank you?

> *"Always try to be a little kinder than is necessary."*
> —J M BARRIE

Around 1980, I read a book that truly inspired me. It triggered a whole movement. It was *Creative Visualization* by Shakti Gawain.

It taught in most basic terms how to use my mind to create images that could become reality. I found it profound.

I wrote the author, in care of her publisher. She wrote back, suggesting I put together a small group of people and she would come to teach us her methods. I'd get to attend free, and she'd give me a percentage of the gate.

I agreed.

It was my first ever seminar. I was naïve. I had no list of contacts, no friends, no influence in Houston, and was truly acting on faith. I figured I would use the methods in Shakti's book and just visualize the event's success. How hard could it be?

Pretty hard, actually. My awkward and impotent attempts to get people to the event were failing.

"How's it going?" Shakti asked, calling me one day.

At the time, I was still sitting in my one room efficiency, broke, deflated, and feeling like a loser. "Not well. I don't have any signups."

Suddenly Shakti snapped. "What!?" she screamed into the phone. Her anger shook me.

"I'm planning to go to Austin as well and they already have the event sold out!"

I didn't know what to say. She was clearly irritated. I mumbled and stuttered, but could not say anything wise or worthwhile.

She hung up on me.

I was cratered. I was hurt. I took on too much, too soon, and didn't know what I was doing. I didn't have any marketing skills. I was still in poverty, trying to act like I wasn't.

Then the phone rang. It was Shakti.

"You okay?" she asked. Her voice was soft, gentle, relaxed.

"Yea," I stammered.

"I did a little meditation, and I can see that we can make this work."

She was loving, kind, and patient. She suggested I contact a few Unity and Unitarian churches and tell them about our little gathering.

I did. And I was able to get people.

When we neared the event date, I went to the airport to pick up Shakti.

"Is there a park or tree area nearby?" she asked.

Turns out she needed to reconnect with nature after being stuck in a metal tube for a few hours. I drove her to Hermann Park in Houston. We parked and went for a short walk.

"This feels good," she said, smiling.

She could tell I was shy, insecure, immature, and at a loss for what to say. She was patient with me.

After our walk, we went to eat, and I asked her questions about her book.

"I wish I had known it was going to be a bestseller," she said. "It was hard to write it. Knowing it was going to be a success would have made the process easier."

She also added something that I still think of today.

"My book is like a child I had," she explained. "I'm not attached to it. I hear about it in the world and I'm proud of it."

Shakti was unexpectedly kind to me.

Decades later, once I was well known in the personal development field, she and I crossed paths via email. I asked if she remembered me. She did.

> *"You cannot do kindness too soon, for you never know how soon it will be too late."*
>
> —RALPH WALDO EMERSON

Struggling was my vocation throughout the 1980s.

The cars I drove—when I owned a car at all—were not dependable. Every time I got in, I never knew if it would start. And if it did, I still didn't know if I would be able to return in it. Breakdowns were normal.

As fortune would have it, a next-door neighbor in Houston was a young man with some skills, like persistence. He would often see me struggling to get my car started and come over and offer to help.

He was bearded, young, and weird. He seemed autistic but was really just so in tune with his connection to nature that he didn't connect with others.

We hit it off.

One day he saw a harmonica sitting on my dashboard. He pointed at it.

"I play it when I'm stuck in traffic," I explained. "You wanna get together and jam?"

"I have no idea what I'm doing," I said. "I just blow through it."

"Let's meet later and see what happens. No pressure. Fun."

Daniel Smith and I met every evening for one entire year. Unless the weather was too cold to sit outside (rare in Texas) or one of us had an emergency (also rare), we met at 7:00 pm sharp at the picnic table in the field across from his house.

He carried a guitar.

I brought my harmonica.

Daniel was kind and patient. He'd play folk songs and urge me to just toot. He encouraged my fun and never noticed (or said anything about) my mistakes.

When I struggled to focus my airflow on a single note on the harmonica, he creatively said maybe I could tape all the other holes closed so I would have to blow through one hole.

It worked.

Even today, decades later, I can play harmonica with passion and control. And I have, on my own albums.

Back then, in the 1980s, I didn't know music or musicians. I could have never predicted that one day I would have a band, or perform on stage, or study with a rock icon, or record fifteen albums. It was everything I could do to jam with Daniel. But it gave me a foundation for music that would later be tapped into.

Daniel and I played on stage once. It was at a bar and I found the experience horrible. The sound system had a delay. I would hear my harmonica seconds after I played it. I felt off, inadequate, and a total failure.

When some woman at the bar said, "I like your harp playing," I walked out in disgust. She had to be lying.

We also recorded a cassette of songs. Daniel had a simple cassette recorder and we played into it. No editing. No overdubs. Daniel was a purist. What we play is what you hear.

I sent it to my father. He loved it and would play it for years, even decades, after we made it.

When my parents drove from Ohio to Texas to meet me and my wife, Daniel and I played a living room concert for them. My dad sat there smiling and tapping his foot. My mother said she loved it. I still remember the moment.

Daniel was beyond eccentric. He would have temper tantrums: he'd begin playing but then get upset about something, usually a fight with his parents, and storm off. No explanation.

But he was like that.

One night he was upset because his dog was barking.

"He's just being a dog," I said.

But Daniel also had natural wisdom.

One day I brought over a new harmonica I had ordered and received.

I played it and didn't like it. I complained.

"Think back to before you got it," Daniel said.

I looked at him.

"What did you feel before you ever received the harmonica?"

"Excited."

"You were excited to get it?"

"Yeah, but now I have it and I don't like it."

"Go back to before you ever got it," he said.

It took me a long time to realize Daniel, in his own way, was urging me to practice gratitude.

I lost track of Daniel during the 1990s, but I've never forgotten his unexpected kindness.

> *"Too often we underestimate the power of a touch,
> a smile, a kind word, a listening ear, an honest
> compliment, or the smallest act of caring, all of
> which have the potential to turn a life around."*
>
> —LEO BUSCAGLIA

Back in the 1980s, way before the internet and instant information, I would buy magazines, read all the ads, and ask for anything that interested me. I was curious about self-help, belief clearing, getting results, and being happier. There were lots of ads for those topics. One of them about clearing beliefs stood out. I don't remember the exact wording, but I do know where it led.

Mandy Evans was behind that ad. She was a counselor specializing in clearing beliefs. She had studied with the same original group who learned the Option Process from its creator, Bruce DiMarsico.

Others in the group included Barry Neil Kaufman, who deeply influenced me with his books, *To Love Is to Be Happy With* and *Son Rise*. I got to meet Bears, as he was called, around 1985, but I didn't have a personal relationship with him. He was too big and too busy. Mandy, however, was approachable.

I bought one of her tapes. I listened to it and was in awe. Her voice and vibe were easy. Her stories were mesmerizing. Her message was mind expanding.

She asked who I could believe if I didn't believe myself.

Wasn't I the one deciding to believe?

If so, wasn't I the authority on my own life?

She opened my mind.

I shared the tape with Larry Andrews, the wealthy businessman who was interested in my life and potential career. He was so taken that he arranged to bring Mandy to Houston for a small event in his home. That's how I got to meet the woman who would continuously change my life for the next few decades, and even today.

Words fail me in describing the impact this lady has on me. We connected from the moment we spoke.

When she arrived in Houston, I drove her to the park. I was still struggling, barely out of poverty, and was embarrassed about where I lived. I didn't have a home, or an apartment. I had a room. And it was tiny, with a TV, hot plate, and toilet all in the same area.

We went to the park, sat on the grass, and talked.

The little group event in my friend's home was smooth, but I felt uneasy, insecure, and immature. I always feared people finding out I knew nothing and was nothing. I had dreams, but in 1985, none of them were profitable. I had nothing to share. Nothing to show.

But Mandy saw something in me she wanted to nourish.

She began giving me counseling sessions. She never charged me. She hasn't charged me still, decades later, and in a new century.

Whether it was my limiting beliefs about money, or the death of my first wife, or conflicting thoughts about being approached by a woman who wanted to seduce me, to fears about failure, to the agony of choosing divorce from my second wife, Mandy was there.

I call her the original Miracles Coach. I created Miracles Coaching because I saw the value of having an ally; but I've always said Mandy is the original coach.

It may be difficult to fathom how much of an impact a single person can have on your life when they are your cheerleader and counselor for almost thirty years.

That's a lifetime.

That's priceless.

I am beyond grateful.

I've always counted on Mandy. She's always invited me to call, any time, for any reason. I've often not called because my belief in needing to do it all myself. But when my face was bruised and my body weary, I called.

And Mandy has always been there, ready with unexpected kindness.

> *"People often ask me what is the most effective technique for transforming their life. It is a little embarrassing that after years and years of research and experimentation, I have to say that the best answer is—just be a little kinder."*
>
> —PIERO FERRUCCI

Mark Joyner hounded me for two years.

He was polite but persistent. He heard of me from Win Wenger, the late genius who taught me and others creativity. Win told Mark that if he wanted to know marketing, see Joe Vitale.

Mark tried. He bought my *Project Phineas* homemade audio program. He bought my early marketing books, such as *Cyberwriting*. He became a fan and wanted to be my digital publisher.

He kept asking for a book from me. Any book. He said he would turn it into what he called an "e-book." He said the future was electronic books, not printed books. He wanted something from me to market to his growing lists.

I resisted—for two years.

I couldn't see anyone wanting a digital book. I was brought up among real books. I read them in real libraries. I bought them in real bookstores. I held them and read them in my very real reality. E-books were not appealing to me.

So I kept telling Mark, "No thanks."

Mark's military background and his skills of persuasion were in play. He never argued. He never stopped. He never made me wrong. He just kept checking in every couple of months, hoping I'd change my mind. I'd say Mark was wisely kind.

Finally, after years of resisting, I sent Mark a copy of my then self-published book, *Hypnotic Writing*. I had printed it at Kinkos and sold it for $50 at classes. It was gas money. I was proud of the book. If Mark wanted to try to sell it as an e-book, then so be it. I sent it and wished him luck. I never expected anything but failure.

Mark wrote a sales letter for my book. I read it and it was so good that I wanted to buy my own book. He put up a website. He sent traffic to it.

I went to bed.

The next morning there were 600 emails in my inbox. At first, I was upset, thinking someone spam bombed me. But as I opened a few emails, I realized they were all receipts. Mark had set up the system so whenever there was an order, I got a copy of it.

Six hundred orders times thirty dollars an order was eighteen thousand dollars.

Overnight.

For a book that wasn't printed, warehoused, packaged, or shipped. It was essentially eighteen thousand dollars clear. And half of that was to me.

I had truly made money while I slept, which is the ideal for most entrepreneurs.

I wrote to Mark and asked, "What else do you want? I have other books."

Over the next few years, Mark sold several e-books for me. I felt like a true kingpin. I found gold in cyber-space.

And when Mark sold his company to Nitro Marketing, and I was picked up by the new owners, Mark assured the buyers that I was a content creating machine. For the next decade, I made products and Nitro sold them online, to our joyous financial success.

Mark's unexpected kindness, in the form of patience and belief, paid off for both of us. We have remained friends and partners for over twenty years. We help each other with brainstorming, product development, and product launches. I am forever grateful for him proving me wrong and making me rich.

> *"We cannot all see alike, but we can all do good."*
>
> —P.T. BARNUM

My first book was published in 1984. It was *Zen and the Art of Writing.*

I quickly learned that publishers rarely know how to market books. They are prestigious printers. My little publisher wasn't even that. He was a guy who fancied publishing books. I'm grateful he believed in my book enough to print 500 copies, but it was soon clear he didn't know what he was doing.

I did a deep dive to learn marketing, copywriting, publicity, advertising, and more. I began applying my newfound knowledge to my little book. Along the way, I learned that a good way to sell books is in the back of the room after speaking.

I resisted that idea. I was introverted, immature, insecure, and terrified of people. Especially a group who were looking at me.

But I faced my fears and began teaching adult education classes on writing. There were only six people in the first class. I perspired my way through it and kept doing it.

The class became popular, and I became better. I sold my book to the audiences. I got clients who hired me to write their book publicity. And I made friends.

One of them was Larry Andrews. He was a powerful, loud, and overweight wealthy man. Somebody discovered oil on his property and Andrews Oil made Larry Andrews rich.

He was also eager to learn. He attended classes, including mine. He bought books, including mine. He took an interest in me, saw something in me that was not yet developed enough for me to see, and encouraged me. We often had lunch, where he mentored me.

"You need more stress," he once told me.

I was stunned. Appalled.

I was in poverty, making pocket change teaching classes and selling books, and stressed out of my mind. He wanted me to add more stress to my life? I couldn't comprehend his advice. Later I would understand that some of the wealthiest people load their schedules and list of goals with an overload of ideas and to-dos. It was actually a secret to success.

Larry introduced me to another wealthy man, Ron McCann, who inherited an air conditioning business. He fancied himself an expert on service. He wanted to have a book but, like many, he didn't want to write it.

Ron hired me to coauthor his book. It was the largest payday of my life. It was the biggest deal of my life. It enabled my wife to buy clothes and me to pay bills. I bought a laptop to write on. I upgraded the car with new tires. It was truly a joyous time.

Larry stayed my advisor and friend throughout my time in Houston. He also wanted to be an author, but he had at least begun his own book. He told me if I helped him complete his book, he'd give me his old personal computer. Up until the laptop I just bought, I had been writing on portable typewriters. I loved my typewriter and in some ways still miss it. You had to really focus when you typed. You can't copy and paste as you can on a computer. I miss the focused intensity of typewriter writing. But I quickly adapted to writing on a computer. Larry gave me his, walked me through how to turn it on, put in a disk (remember, this was around 1992), and fire it up. A few hours after playing with the computer,

I wrote a little booklet that became a massive success. *Turbocharge Your Writing* was a booklet of only sixteen pages, but a printer I knew published it for nothing, knowing I would publicly give him credit. And the little book became *Hypnotic Writing*, which I sold in the back of the room after talks. It also became my first e-book, and an impressive success online.

Larry was wise, kind, and experienced. When his brother and me attended the Landmark Forum self-help seminar and both felt it was a waste of time, Larry met with us to discuss our disappointment.

"It was a waste," I said.

"It was just egos strutting on stage," his brother said. Larry looked at us, reflecting.

"The seminar has been around over ten years," he began. "It's designed to help people get results. It's worked for tens of thousands of people. The reason it may not have worked for you two is you may not have wanted it to work."

I gasped.

"If you want to stay stuck," Larry explained. "You'll find fault with everyone and everything, instead of allowing the opportunity for change."

I never forgot Larry's insight. It made me realize that some people—even me—unconsciously choose to complain in order to remain the same.

I recently tried to find Larry online. He's not listed on Facebook and I don't see any listings for him. His unexpected kindness to me helped me during a dark time. I would like to thank him yet again.

> *"The simplest acts of kindness are by far more powerful than a thousand heads bowing in prayer."*
>
> —MAHATMA GANDHI

One of the best books I ever read was *The Great Brain Robbery* by Ray Considine and Murray Raphel around 1987.

I was on a quest to learn marketing. I was chewing up everything I could find in any library or bookstore. Discovering the works of these two authors, and particularly this book, was a turning point.

I always wondered how creative people came up with ideas. How entrepreneurs came up with new businesses. How millionaires and billionaires were able to think so big. I felt stupid and incompetent, but reading stories of how regular people solved problems helped teach me how to think differently.

It was like learning a new language. At first it makes no sense. You feel inadequate. But as you keep hearing it, it begins to make sense. Soon you are speaking the language too.

I was so taken by the authors that I wrote Murray a fan letter. I was struggling. Unknown. But eager. Sincere.

And hungry. He saw something in me and sent me not only a letter, but an entire box of his products.

Books. Videos. Articles. It was joyous to open such a huge box of presents. Murray gave from his heart. He didn't ask for anything. There was no bill. No request. He was giving.

I haven't thought of him in decades. I just went online and did a search. Not only is Murray still with us and working, but now he's a playwright. It looks like he sold his marketing business and that he's attached to Syracuse University. I tried to reach him on LinkedIn and Facebook to remind him of his kindness to me and to thank him again, but his contact info appears locked. I ordered what looks like his autobiography, *Murray Raphel Remembers*.

Whatever is in his book, in my heart is Murray and his unexpected kindness to an unknown writer.

> *"How do we change the world?*
> *One random act of kindness at a time."*
> —MORGAN FREEMAN

Back in the late 1980s and 1990s, I was devouring books on marketing, advertising, copywriting, and more. When my first book came and went in 1984, I knew I had to learn marketing or I'd never be noticed. Nor would anything I wrote. One of the prolific authors back then was Jeffrey Lant. His mammoth books helped lots of people, including me.

One day he offered a chance to have an ad in a card deck that would be mailed to his clients and book buyers. I took a page from Lant's book and felt this was a great opportunity. I paid one thousand dollars—which I had to borrow—and placed an ad that offered "A Free Personalized Marketing Strategy" from me.

The ad was solid copy. The offer was pretty irresistible. When someone wrote back, I sent them a prewritten general marketing plan, personalized with their name and a few tips based on what business they said they were in. I truly personalized every report. I invited them to write to me (no email back then) if they wanted to talk about me implementing the strategy.

I didn't hear from many people, but one man changed my life forever.

Jim Chandler and I spoke. He was from Ohio, same as me. He went to Kent State University, same as me. He was into writing, publishing, and marketing, same as me. We were like two lost brothers who finally found each other.

Jim wanted to be a publisher. I wanted one of my books published. We created a win-win. Jim published my book, *The Seven Lost Secrets of Success*. I helped him with ads for it, publishing advice, and marketing documents, like sales letters.

It was the beginning of success for me as an author. The book was well received and well-reviewed. And I found out I was pretty good in interviews. One group of salespeople heard me interviewed on a radio show as they were leaving town. They stopped the car, turned around, and went to the bookstore where I was later doing a book signing. They all bought books.

Another time I was interviewed by the president of a multi-level marketing company. He so loved my answers, he bought almost 20,000 copies of my book. It was miraculous. And it was one of the first nice paydays of my writing career. The profit helped me travel to Australia when I went the first time. And the book sales introduced me to tens of thousands of new people.

If it weren't for Jim, I'm not sure how much longer the world would have taken to notice me as an author. I was crawling up but I hadn't arrived. Jim's unexpected kindness gave me the boost in confidence and notoriety I needed. I stay in contact with Jim even today. I am forever grateful for his unexpected kindness.

> *"To touch someone with kindness*
> *is to change someone forever."*
> —MIKE DOOLEY

Back when I was looking at ads in the back of new age magazines, circa 1980s and 1990s, I saw a funky looking one for a book about new beginnings. It was the teachings of Abraham.

The authors were Jerry and Esther Hicks. But calling them "authors" was a stretch, as the information they wrote down came from an other-worldly source.

I wrote and asked for a review copy of the book. Back then I got paid $25 for a book review. I wanted the book for free, and the check for survival.

The book was so poorly produced that it was a type-written manuscript printed and bound. It wasn't pretty. But energy around the book captivated me. I read it and wrote the authors. It turns out they were in Texas, too.

Jerry called me and we had a great time. He had a clear voice and energetic presence. He asked questions about book marketing. By then I was becoming an expert on the subject.

He hired me to write a full-page ad, back cover copy, and an introduction for the first children's book, Sara.

We met at Carmel Temple, a small church in Houston. I knew the couple running the place. I had spoken there myself, one time right after Jose Silva.

Jerry and Esther came to speak. We had an awesome connection. We had lunch afterwards. I felt close to both. I found them to be the nicest people I had ever met. I mean, ever. They were a joy to be around.

They hired me for monthly publicity. I would write news releases and send them out.

They needed a website, so I introduced them to my web guy.

As the Hicks began to grow, their little family run shop couldn't handle all the orders. They asked me for advice on software that could process tens of thousands of orders a month. They were getting bigger than any mainstream publisher.

Jerry called me one day and said he had an idea for an unusual calendar.

"There are two columns on the front," he explained. "One for your to-do list and the other for the Universe's to-do list. On the back would be a quote from Abraham."

He wanted to know who would or could print it. I still think it's the best idea and best calendar ever devised. I still tell people about the two to-do lists today.

They invited me to attend a seminar they were holding in San Antonio. Afterwards, I went with a small group to visit their home.

I included Jerry and Esther in this book because I always found them to be loving and supportive of me. So many people in the new age community are flaky. Not the Hicks. They were clear headed, had integrity, and treated me with great respect. Some of the clients I worked with didn't have that respect for me. So when I got it from Jerry and Esther, I regarded it as unexpected kindness.

Jerry has passed away, but Esther continues her work channeling Abraham. I love them and will always be grateful for them. The teachings of Abraham alone greatly inspired me and helped me lead a happier life.

> *"You can always give something,*
> *even if it is just kindness."*
>
> —ANNE FRANK

One of the best books I read in the 1980s about negotiating, persuasion, and selling, was *Secrets of Power Negotiating* by Roger Dawson. I was enthralled. The book was brilliant and beautifully written. I was so impressed that I wrote the author a letter of congratulations. To my surprise, he wrote back. That was kind in itself, but he said he was going to be in Houston and invited me to attend his lecture.

I was driving a big, dirty, clunky, and undependable car. I was still living in that one room dump. But I put on a sports jacket I bought from Goodwill, got in the car, and urged it to the event in Houston. I wanted to meet Roger.

He smiled big, gave me a handshake, and invited me to sit.

"They didn't sell out, but it's a good crowd," he said.

He held the audience with his British accent and charming stories.

He seemed relaxed and confident, professional and persuasive.

After his talk, he stood by a table with his books and tape sets for sale.

"I'll give you my recent tapes from Nightingale-Conant," he said.

I started to take a set off the table but he stopped me.

"Wait. I'll give you one afterwards. I want people to think the sets are scarce, so I only leave one on the table at a time."

Point taken. I was learning.

I offered to give him a ride to the airport after the event. He accepted. Of course, he didn't know I was driving a Flintstone mobile. When I pulled up in my car after he checked out, he said, "The hotel can get me a ride."

"I'd like to do it," I said.

Roger agreed, which was another act of kindness.

On the trip, I told him I wanted to be a success too. I told him of my efforts to get into Nightingale-Conant. I told him I was trying to be a published author. I confessed that I felt stuck and confused.

"You always have a choice," he told me.

"It doesn't feel like it."

"There is always another way," he persisted.

"I feel lost," I continued. "I don't know how to break into success with anything unique."

"Create a Vitale Method," he advised.

I didn't understand.

"There's nothing new anywhere. You just rename things. My persuasion program is basically from Aristotle."

"I love your book," I said.

"I didn't write it," he said.

"You didn't?"

"Ghostwriter did it. I'm a better speaker than a writer."

I was floored. Stunned. Disappointed. Being an aspiring writer, I longed to find writing I admired and authors who mastered the art of it. I thought Roger was such a gem. Learning he didn't write his own book truly dropped the bottom out of me.

But he was honest with me. I was always grateful that Roger gave so much of his time to a nobody. There were no signs that I would ever be a success. Yet Roger treated me with respect and offered his advice to me with no request. Even confessing the authorship of his book was said to educate me, not frustrate or disappoint me. He was trying to help.

Almost two decades later, I was in the studios of Nightingale-Conant recording yet another program. Roger's name came up. I told the engineer the entire story of how Roger was nice to me long ago.

"Let's make a video for him."

We did. Right there. The camera came on and I made a short video of thanks for Roger. I never heard if he received or watched it, but I made it and we sent it.

> *"When words are both true and kind,
> they can change the world."*
> —BUDDHA

A healer I'll call Jonathan redirected my life with his gift of coaching me. I'm not sure how we met; perhaps it was a gathering in Houston where he approached me. He told me he helped people get past their blocks. When I asked him to explain, he couldn't. But he invited me to have a session with him at no charge.

I was broke and desperate. I couldn't say no and was learning a secret to success was in saying yes. Jonathan and I were moved in my first session with him. He "got" that he was never to charge me, but was to continue working with me. I got blown away by energy torpedoing through my body and up my spine.

Jonathan and I worked together, weekly, for years. We would meet, talk about whatever was on our minds, clear what we could verbally, and then shut our eyes, sit back, and invite divine energy to correct our inner pathways. An hour or two later, we'd "awaken." Then we'd go eat a Thai lunch that made us both smile.

As I worked with Jonathan, my career began to take off. I was unknown, struggling, living in a dump, and driving a clunker when we started. After spending time with him, I was published, making a name for myself as an online marketer, bought an owner-financed home, and was driving my first new car.

I'm sad to say Jonathan is long gone from my life. His unexpected kindness taught me the value of getting clear of inner energy blocks. I am forever grateful.

> *"You can accomplish by kindness what you cannot by force."*
>
> —PUBLILIUS SYRUS

As I learned marketing and applied it to my own books, other authors sought me out. One guardian angel in flesh form was a man who could walk on water. In fact, one of his books was *When You Can Walk on Water, Take the Boat.*

John Harricharan was a loving, sincere, articulate, spiritual teacher and speaker from South America, and of Indian descent. I loved his voice and vibe the first time we spoke on the phone. He was considered a psychic, but he never liked the label. He was simply intuitive, like all of us.

At the time, I was longing to attract the coolest car I could imagine: a BMW Z3. I had seen one on the highway in Houston once and froze in desire. I told John about it.

"The car is coming to you," he would say. "It'll be yours soon."

I helped John with his marketing, and he helped me with life decisions, like leaving my first wife.

She wanted to be alone. She even encouraged me to date and look for a new partner. It was confusing and frightening. John was there for me, as well as for my wife. His advice comforted me. And her.

Throughout the separation and later divorce, John was there for both of us. He gave with such unexpected kindness that I still marvel at his generosity today.

One day I met him for lunch in Atlanta, before speaking at his own event.

"Look at me," I said. "I'm in the room with one of the greatest spiritual teachers of our time."

John looked around the room.

"I'm talking about YOU," I told him.

John was so humble that he didn't realize the hyperbolic comment was a truth, and it was about him.

He was very wise. Here are some of his quotes:

"The subconscious reacts very quickly to strong emotions or feelings. Whatever it is you vividly imagine, the subconscious thinks is actually happening. The subconscious, if instructed properly, is like a faithful, obedient servant who fulfills your every wish."

And . . .

"If you do not feel you deserve good things, subconsciously, you will do all within your power to punish yourself by not getting those good things. So the feeling of deserving is a very important thing."

And . . .

"Fear cannot exist in the presence of faith. Fear only exists because you feel that you are not in control. Give up the need to be in control, take a leap in faith, and fear will vanish as the mists in the morning sun."

We stayed in touch as my first wife passed, my relationship with a woman who became my second wife grew, and as I attracted my BMW Z3 (and then many more cars over the years).

John also introduced me to the man who would change my life and finances forever.

One of John's clients and friends said, "If I could meet anyone, I'd love to meet Joe Vitale."

"No problem," said John. "I'll make a call."

He did. And there began a relationship that is still alive and well today, with Frank Mangano and his company, Statbrook. Frank and his family became dear friends. And every time we met or talked, we also thought of John.

Sadly, John is gone now. But I've never forgotten his unexpected kindness to me, my wife, and to Frank.

In our minds, he truly did walk on water.

> *"How far that little candle throws his beams!*
> *So shines a good deed in a weary world."*
> —WILLIAM SHAKESPEARE

Barney Zick was a giant. He was tall, overweight, had a big voice, a large presence, and he commanded attention. He was a speaker and consultant. He was successful in real estate in Houston. He published books and released audios. He heard one of my breakfast talks at a meeting in Houston. He liked me.

"I have an opportunity for you," he told me one day over lunch.

"Say more."

"PBS television is willing to have you speak to a small group about marketing. They'll film it with their huge cameras and give you the master tape."

I was naïve and didn't see the benefit of doing this, except for experience and exposure.

"Any pay?"

"No," he said. "But they'll film your talk and that's worth about twelve thousand dollars. You can then make copies of it and sell the talk, use it to get paid speaking gigs, and more."

I was sold.

I went home to my rinky-dink one room living space and became obsessed. I wanted my presentation to knock people out. I found copies of old ads, made graphs for the overhead projector, and prepared myself. While I was essentially broke and near penniless, I had a credit card.

I bought an $800 suit. I wanted to look good. It was the most I had ever spent on clothes. My logic said if this was being filmed, it might live forever.

There were less than twenty people in the studio. And the cameras were the old kind used to film TV shows. I did my best to not be distracted by them moving around. I was clearly nervous, as I poured sweat as I spoke. But I gave a good presentation, and you can still see it today, almost thirty years later. It's on YouTube.

Barney was right. I later had an introduction edited into the filmed presentation, and made it a complete product. It was my course on Marketing That Sells. People like Mark Joyner and numerous others would later buy it. It established me as an authority on marketing.

I'm sad to say Barney died in 2005. He never saw my star shoot into orbit. He was a great giver in my professional life. He advised on my business card, my talks, and my future. I miss him and his unexpected kindness.

> *"Many men fail because they do not see the importance of being kind and courteous to the men under them. Kindness to everybody always pays for itself. And, besides, it is a pleasure to be kind."*
>
> —CHARLES M. SCHWAB

As I've mentioned, a secret to success is having someone believe in you almost more than you believe in yourself.

One of the people who did that for me in the early 1990s was a woman who attended one of my adult learning classes.

She asked to have lunch with me.

I was jogging at the time and developed enormous heel spurs. They were incredibly painful. I remember limping into the salad bar restaurant to meet Louise Dewey. After we said our hellos, she shocked me with her unexpected and kind offer.

"I'm a widow," she told me. "My husband left me a little money. I don't have much, but I'd like to sponsor an event for you."

I didn't know why or how and could barely keep up with her stunning offer.

"An event?"

"I think you are going places," she said. "You need to go bigger than the adult education service. It's given you training and exposure, but you need your own event."

My classes were tiny, less than ten people for the first few years. When I ran a meditation center for a while, I would draw a handful more. But I wasn't doing much as an event promoter or leader.

"What would the event be about?" I asked.

"Whatever you want."

We talked more. I was mostly confused. Louise was offering me an opportunity and I didn't feel ready for it.

"You can pay me back from the event proceeds," she said. "And if it doesn't work, I'll write off the funds. But I think it will work."

I never took her up on her offer. I was too insecure.

I was too afraid.

I was too into thinking nothing worked out for me, so why would this?

But I never forgot Louise or her unexpected kindness.

I'm still in contact with her. She has attended virtually every event I've ever held in Texas. She volunteers at my events.

And I've introduced her and told the story of how she believed in me more than I did. Because of Louise and her confidence in me, I slowly stepped out into the world as an author, speaker, and leader.

But way back in Houston, limping through life, listening to a woman offer to help me and my career, I just didn't feel ready to say yes.

Today I know that a secret to success is to say yes—even when you have no idea how to do what you are being asked to do.

Ultimately, our saying yes to the big goal helps us grow into the person who can manifest the big goal.

But I didn't know that when Louise first approached me. Fortunately, she has remained as an angel and supporter in my life, still practicing unexpected kindness.

> *"Shall we make a new rule of life from tonight:*
> *always to try to be a little kinder than is necessary?"*
>
> —JAMES BARRIE

Back when I was looking at classified ads in the back of new age magazines, I spotted one selling a tape called, "Rationalization Therapy." It may have cost five dollars. While I was broke, I always invested in learning materials. This felt like a turning point. I bought it.

The cassette was a humorous look at how we rationalize everything we do, right down to the most ridiculous. But along with the tape was another audio. The gentleman who made the tape, sent me an audio message. He also invited me to make one for him.

He would become my audio pen pal for the next ten years. I still remember the first tape I made for him. I was living in the run-down room, broke, desperate, unhappy, but curious. My voice was shaky and uncertain. I felt insecure. But I wanted to make a tape. It sounded like fun.

I made it and sent it. My new friend made a tape in return. Slowly, over time, we began sending each other weekly cassettes. We talked about the books we read, the tapes we listened to, the self-help gurus, and their methods. The more I made the tapes, the more comfortable I became. Before long, I was recording ranting and raving while driving through the streets of Houston. I was uninhibited, improvisational, opinionated, and having a blast.

It would be almost twenty years before I met the mysterious man. He lived in Nashville. I went there to have one of my new music albums mastered by a Grammy winner who mastered at least one album by Neil Diamond. While there, I arranged to have coffee with Scott.

Scott Hammaker was a delight.

"Because of you," I told him, "I can talk in public. Those ten years of making tapes in the car helped me relax as a speaker. Now I get on stage and feel comfortable speaking."

It was true. I learned how to speak, to be entertaining, and be educational because of that decade of creating audio tapes for Scott. His tapes back to me gave me feedback and encouragement. My continuing to make tapes for him were rehearsals for a life on stage I never knew I would have.

I doubt Scott really felt my sincerity. But I wanted to thank him for his unexpected kindness.

> *"Wherever there is a human being,*
> *there is an opportunity for a kindness."*
> —SENECA

Trying to be a published author was a long journey that led me to being homeless and then in poverty. I kept struggling but I kept trying.

Along the way, around 1990, I discovered Bob Bly and his books, in particular, *Secrets of a Freelance Writer*. That book awakened me to different ways I could make money from writing. More than that, it introduced me to a long-distance mentor who gave me unexpected kindness—repeatedly.

After reading Bob's book, I wrote to him. He wrote back, answering my questions, and telling me about his other books. I loved his personal touch. I still have most of those letters. I read his other reports, and other books, and applied all I was learning. I was able to become a copywriter due to Bob's advice. Being a copywriter led to my making money from my writing—finally.

Bob and I stayed in touch. When I got my first book deals around 1995, I called and asked for his advice. I didn't have an agent. Bob was kind and took time to help me. I never forgot it.

When the internet went public, and I was seen as an online marketing pioneer, Bob wrote me, asking for advice on how to sell online. I loved the karma of it all. I asked him for advice pre-internet. He asked me for advice post-internet. We both practiced unexpected kindness to the other.

Years later, in a new century and still before *The Secret* was to shake the world, I went to New York City where Bob invited me to dinner. He was a delight. I learned he loved books more than anything, just like me. And he loved writing, just like me. He also loved horror movies, unlike me. But I guess if we weren't different in some key ways, one of us wouldn't be needed.

I'm still friends with Bob and I'm still inspired by him. People marvel when they hear I've written eighty books. I marvel when I hear Bob has written over one hundred books—with more coming. But it's all relative. Bob always pointed out that Isaac Asimov wrote or edited more than 500 books. I feel like a slacker compared to either of them.

> *"Whatever possession we gain by our sword cannot be sure or lasting, but the love gained by kindness and moderation is certain and durable."*
>
> —ALEXANDER THE GREAT

Around 1997, I started receiving emails from a stranger asking questions about my forthcoming book on P.T. Barnum.

I had researched and written about the great circus showman. I dug deep into his life and career to unearth his strategies for success. I was very much into marketing at the time, and regard Barnum as a marketing genius. I was honored and excited to release my book, *There's a Customer Born Every Minute.*

Since I was so excited about my project, answering questions from a stranger was an extension of my joy. I was glad to reply. I was glad to help. The strange man kept writing, asking very astute questions. It was clear he was sincere. I was happy to answer.

But then something shocking happened. First, a little back story.

I had wanted to be produced by Nightingale-Conant (NC) for a decade. They were the greatest self-help audio producers in history. They recorded and promoted the legends, from Zig Ziglar and Napoleon Hill to Denis Waitley and Wayne Dyer. I wanted to be one of their authors.

When my book on Bruce Barton was published, *The Seven Lost Secrets of Success*, I sent it to NC. I felt in my bones this was a match for their audience. But they rejected me. And they rejected every other idea I had.

It was devastating; horribly disappointing.

But I never let go of my dream of being an NC author.

The stranger who kept asking me about Barnum one day sent me an email that turned my life around.

"Thank you for answering my questions about Barnum. My name is Peter Wink. By the way, if you ever want your material considered by Nightingale-Conant, I am their senior marketing manager."

Gasp.

I still remember the moment.

I still remember the shock.

I must have stared at my computer screen for days. Or so it seemed. Of course, I wrote back to Pete, told him my dream, and offered to send him my books. He gave me their address, and I overnighted a crate of stuff to him.

Pete then went to bat for me. He asked for more copies of my books. I sent them and he took them and placed one on every desk in the NC offices.

I had a homemade tape set at the time, and I sent that too. Pete loved it and thought it could be a winner if professionally recorded in NC's studios in Chicago. He went to sell the team.

But it wasn't an easy sell.

The decision makers weren't as convinced of me or my work as Pete. They declined. But Pete didn't give up. He talked about me at every meeting. He put more copies of my work on every desk.

And when Christmas came around, Pete took down the star of David at the top of the tree and replaced it with my photo. Not only that, he put photos of me in every bathroom in their offices.

Finally, the managers decided to give me a shot. Pete helped me negotiate my contract. The advance was low abut he said don't worry. I'll hire you to write the sales letter to market your program. He did. Between the deal for the new audio program, and the pay for the copywriting, I came off pretty well.

Plus, I was finally being published by NC.

My program was *The Power of Outrageous Marketing*. It became a huge success right out of the gate. Despite that, NC didn't invite me to record another program until after the movie *The Secret* came out, and after the company began to suffer in overall sales.

When I returned about seven years later, it was to record what became NC's all-time greatest bestseller, *The Missing Secret*.

I love NC and am proud of my various programs with them. But none of them would have happened without the kindness of a man who wrote to me asking about P.T. Barnum.

> *"It is the characteristic of the magnanimous man to
> ask no favor but to be ready to do kindness to others."*
> —ARISTOTLE

went to Australia in 1998 due to a missing comma.

Back then, my email list was small, and I personally wrote back to anyone who wrote to me first.

One day I received an email that simply said, "Beautiful Joe. I loved your recent newsletter."

Anyone who called me beautiful was worth a follow-up.

The writer meant "Beautiful, Joe," but the missing comma made it a compliment.

I wrote back.

It turns out the person was a woman named Alicia. She lived in Australia. She didn't know I had wanted to visit Australia for years. We began a correspondence.

Alicia was an actress, or at least a wannabee. She and her husband lived in Melbourne. They invited me over, saying they would act as my tour guide. I was interested.

My book, *The Seven Lost Secrets of Success*, had just sold well and I had a little money. My first wife didn't want to go.

Even though domestic flight travel was rare for me at that time and I had never experienced international travel, I boarded a plane and began the long adventure overseas, to meet complete strangers.

I had never been on so many flights. Or such lengthy flights. Or to an entirely different country. What comforted me was knowing Alicia would be there to greet me. Even though we had never met, we had enough of a correspondence for me to trust her.

She and her husband met me at the airport. She was an Amazon size muscular blonde. Stunningly beautiful. Her husband was short and stocky and had a riotous sense of humor. They both welcomed me and offered to take me to dinner.

They had planned my entire weeklong stay. They had tours and reservations. Neither had much money but they were pulling out all the stops.

"You are like Wayne Dyer to us."

I was years away from any fame from being in *The Secret* or for any self-help books. I was yet to realize the internet and my presence on it was making me a celebrity of sorts.

One restaurant they took me to in Little Italy of Melbourne was so unforgettably delicious that we went back to it three times in five days.

Giovanni Ricco was an Elvis lookalike, only Italian and speaking with an Australian accent. He knew how to entertain.

He sang at tables.

He danced.

He took a liking to me. He told me about Italy and urged me to go there.

"Something great will happen for you when you go there," he said. "Go. You need to go."

Giovanni made sure I was stuffed. No portion control. No single portions. Every meal was Sunday with the family over in terms of saturation and satisfaction.

One evening he had fed and watered me so much that I mumbled a need for a taxi.

"A what?"

"I can't walk," I said. "Get me a ride to our motel."

He did. And I still remember the next morning's headache.

I still think of Giovanni today, decades later. But what I've never forgotten was the unexpected kindness of Alicia and her husband.

With or without a comma.

> *"Kindness extended, received, or observed*
> *beneficially impacts the physical health*
> *and feelings of everyone involved."*
>
> —WAYNE DYER

Bob Proctor redirected my life with an act of kindness I wasn't prepared to accept. At least I thought I wasn't. Good thing I didn't stop him, or I may not be writing these words today.

It was back in 1999. I'm making a name for myself as a copywriter, marketer, and internet entrepreneur. My books for the American Marketing Association and American Management Association were out. My first audio program with Nightingale-Conant was out. A buzz was about. People were turning to me for advice.

One man sent me a check for $20,000, hiring me to write news releases for him before we ever met. And Bob Proctor invited me to his seminar in Denver.

Bob was already a legend. He was the Napoleon Hill of our times. He was a no-nonsense speaker about setting goals and attaining them. He ate little, drank nothing, always wore a double-breasted suit, and never had a hair out of place. He knew his mission. He was dedicated to helping people. He heard of me and wanted to meet me. I flew to Denver to see him.

To thank him for his generosity, I gave him a copy of a then unpublished booklet I had written but never shared in public. *Spiritual Marketing* was written for my sister. I had gone from homeless to somebody and knew some steps to success. I put them in the little booklet. I thought it might be a cool gift for Bob, so I printed a copy at Kinkos, and brought it to him.

I wasn't prepared for what happened. Bob read it.

"I love this booklet of yours," he said. "I'd like to publish it."

He then went on stage in front of his crowd of three hundred souls and said something shocking.

"Joe Vitale is in the audience, folks," he said. "He gave me his newest book. You'll all want it. It's called *Spiritual Marketing.*"

I felt the energy wave across the room. Ohs and ahs of recognition. And at the first break, people mobbed me, wanting the book. I had to explain the book didn't exist yet. Only Bob had a copy.

"I'll publish the book," a man said, explaining he was a publisher.

"You haven't seen the book!"

"Bob has," he countered. "He likes it. That's good enough for me."

My head was spinning. Bob wanted to publish the book. This stranger wanted to publish the book. I wasn't ready to publish the book. I thought it revealed my interest in woo-woo, which could kill my growing recognition as a marketer. But I couldn't pass up the signs urging me to proceed.

I went with the publisher in the audience. He was using the then new print on demand service. It was a publishing bakery. An order came in, a book was printed. No warehouse. No inventory. A brilliant way to get a book in print without much if any upfront cost.

The *New York Times* wrote a story on the new way to get published. They mentioned me and my book. That boosted sales. *Spiritual Marketing* became my first Amazon bestseller. Not number one, but certainly in the top fifty or less.

Then a larger publisher contacted me. Wiley wanted to print my book, but they wanted a different title. I went to my mastermind at the time, and we conjured up the title, *The Attractor Factor*. I used every trick in the book to make it number one. And it hit the spot, beating all books, including the latest from Harry Potter's JK Rowling and the late Pope.

But the story didn't stop there.

A woman in Australia called me. Said she was thinking of making a movie on the Law of Attraction. She read *The Attractor Factor* and wondered if I would be in her film. Of course, it was *The Secret*, and the rest is history.

Bob and I stayed in touch over the decades. We spoke together in Peru. It was the largest live audience I'd ever been in front of: 20,000 people. I had a police escort, bodyguard, translator, and entourage. The only other speaker on the bill was Bob. It was a highlight of my life.

Let me tell you a couple of random stories I remember about Bob.

He called me when I lived in Houston and was becoming a marketer and speaker on the "small circuit" of that city. My answering machine back then said, "I'm busy helping someone become rich and famous. You can be next. Leave a message."

Bob called my number three times, playing it for anyone near his office. When he finally got me on the phone, he asked, "Are you rich?"

"Not even close."

"You've never actually focused on money, have you?" I admitted no.

"Have you read *Think and Grow Rich*?" I had.

"Read it again," he said. "I read it every day and have since 1967."

Another time he asked me if I flew first class.

"No, I can't afford it."

"That's why you can't afford it."

"I'm sorry?"

"Flying first class is an act of prosperity thinking," he explained. "You have to fly first class to tell yourself you are worthy of prosperity."

It took me two years, at least, to start flying first class. Every time I flew coach, I felt broke. Bob's wisdom kept shaking me. When I finally flew first class, my self-esteem went up. So did my prosperity. I only fly first class or private jet now.

I'm sad to report that Bob died in early 2022. I didn't get him on my online TV show, and I regret it. But I did thank him, many times. He would always chuckle, delighted that he had a hand in upgrading my career.

All from Bob Proctor's act of kindness.

> *"No act of kindness, no matter how small,*
> *is ever wasted."*
>
> —AESOP

The man who sold the Brooklyn Bridge gave my career a turbo lift in the 1990s.

I was still struggling but making a name for myself as a copywriter. Due to my book *Hypnotic Writing*, people wanted to hire me to write sales letters and ads. Due to my book on Barnum, *There's a Customer Born Every Minute*, well respected entrepreneurs were contacting me.

Paul Hartunian was watching TV one day when he saw the bridge being torn up and replaced. He drove to the site and asked if he could haul off the wood for them. They needed it removed, so Paul hauled it away. But then he cut it into squares, created a placard, and sold the pieces. He sent out news releases saying he sold the Brooklyn Bridge. He got the media to run the story. He even went on Johnny Carson.

Paul heard of me and wanted to meet. He was coming to Houston. I met him for dinner. Three hours later, my life was changed forever.

Everything Paul told me to do, I did.

Quit answering the phone. Get an answering machine or service.

Quit speaking for free. Charge every time you get on stage.

Create an audio product. Just put pillows under the cracks in the door, turn on a cassette recorder, and talk. No studio needed. No editing needed. "As long as you tell people it is rough and unedited, they won't complain."

I obeyed and did it all. I created an audio program called *Project Phineas*, named after P.T. Barnum. I charged $500 for it, as Paul said it needed to be high ticket. I sold that program, traded it for products and services I wanted, and used it as my prototype to get in the good graces of Nightingale-Conant. It was truly the rough cut of what became the polished, *The Power of Outrageous Marketing*.

Paul also hired me to write the sales letter for his audio program on dating. I wrote and rewrote that copy until even Michelangelo would be impressed. I wanted to satisfy Paul and I did. He loved it.

He also began sending clients to me: Authors who wanted publicity and musicians needing a media bump. Paul told me to charge $5,000 to write news releases. It was a preposterous sum for me to ask for at the time, but I knew Paul was my unpaid mentor. I wanted to acknowledge his wisdom. I wanted to be a success like him.

Paul's true love was dogs. He would raise money for shelters by saying, "donate $1,000, and we'll name a dog after you." My first wife, Marian, loved animals too. So I donated $1,000, and Paul named a dog, "Marian." It was a smart and kind thing to do for me, for Paul, and for Marian.

> *"Assume the feeling of the wish fulfilled."*
> —NEVILLE GODDARD

Before the internet, one of my favorite ways to find old books was browsing used bookstores.

I loved the hunt. I relished wandering aisles, looking at dusty old books. I celebrated finding rare books in self-help or metaphysics, marketing, or copywriting, as others celebrate football game wins.

The movie *The Secret* hadn't come out yet, and wouldn't for decades, so the masses didn't know about some of the books I was finding. They weren't interested in the Law of Attraction yet, or any of the metaphysical authors who started the movement in the 1800s and early 1900s.

I slowly acquired a nice library of gems. I always imagined the authors of these volumes as practicing unexpected kindness, because they shared their wisdom and experience to an audience they would never meet, even to future generations.

Authors such as Elizabeth Towne, who was like an early century Louise Hay, writing and publishing others (like *The Science of Getting Rich* by Wallace Wattles or *Your Invisible Power* of Genevieve Behrend).

Some of these deceased authors so lit up my heart with their forgotten words that I republished them, such as Behrend's lost classic, *Attaining Your Desires* and Neville's first book, *At Your Command*.

I could write about numerous authors, gone now, who influenced me. They were ghosts alive in their writings, speaking to me from the time machine called books.

Take Neville.

I never met Neville Goddard. He passed away in 1972, right after I left high school, and before my adventures through homelessness and poverty began. But because Neville left recordings of his talks, and his many self-published books, his unusual wisdom guided me, changed me, and redirected my life.

I probably discovered his material circa 1995. No one knew who he was then. Because I read so much, and follow "breadcrumbs" as I read, I was led to this modern-day mystic.

I began collecting his books and slowly built a library of books autographed by him. I also found cassettes of his talks. And two phonograph records of his presentations.

Most of this was easy to find, and affordable, because he yet hadn't reached critical mass in popular appeal. I'm told part of his global fame came from me, as I referenced Neville in my own books, such as *Spiritual Marketing*, aka *The Attractor Factor*.

I found Neville's first book, *At Your Command*. I paid over five hundred dollars for it. I was so taken by the simplicity of it that I republished the book.

A small publisher at the time, just getting started in the publishing world, offered to print the book at no charge to me. I accepted. And because I was becoming a marketer, I added a sales letter to the book, offering some of my own books as an upsell.

Neville practiced unexpected kindness in his life.

I'm told he let people record his talks. He'd be on stage and there would be a dozen or more reel to reel tape recorders at his feet. He gave away his wisdom.

He self-published his books but never enforced any copyright restrictions that I was aware of. Consequently, his books and audios are readily available today, more so than they were to me in 1995, or even 2005, when I published his book, *At Your Command*.

"Assumption hardens into fact," was one of his key phrases.

He signed many of his books, "Assume the feeling of the wish fulfilled."

His advice was to act from the end result; meaning, instead of visualizing what you want as happening one day in the future, pretend it already happened and feel the reality of it now.

Decades later I would record a song with Grammy nominated singer Ruthie Foster, called "Feel It Real," to reinforce Neville's message.

He also said, "Capture the feeling associated with your realized wish by assuming the feeling that would be yours were you already in possession of the thing you desire, and your wish will objectify itself."

Today, you can find books by and about Neville readily available. Old copies of his original works, sometimes autographed, can be seen on eBay. His audios, and transcripts, are all online today.

Neville left a body of work that was, for me and millions of others, an act of unexpected kindness.

> *"Perhaps you will forget the kind words*
> *you say today, but the recipient may*
> *cherish them over a lifetime."*
>
> —DALE CARNEGIE

Before *The Secret* came out, one of my early clients for book publicity turned out to be a magician.

Scott Lewis knew everyone in Vegas because he was the chiropractor to the stars. Through him, I got to meet Lance Burton and Marshall Brodein and other legends of magic. Thanks to Scott, I attended my first ever magic convention. It was in Vegas. Stars of my youth were there, like Mark Wilson. And a truly charming man by the name of John Booth was there. I'll never forget meeting him.

"Are you a magician?" Booth asked me.

He had the old school good looks of early Hollywood. His smile lit up the room. His eyes were focused on me. He was truly present. Despite the crowds of people around us, John Booth made me feel like I was the most important person at the event. He asked for my business card and I handed it to him. He studied it a moment.

"May I keep this?" he asked.

You have no idea how flattering it was to have this living legend of magic ask if he could keep my card. Obviously business cards are made to be dispersed. I had plenty. But the fact that he asked made me and my card feel important.

I collected every book by John Booth. I will always remember him and his unexpected kindness to me.

> *"Kindness can become its own motive.*
> *We are made kind by being kind."*
> —ERIC HOFFER

The other magician I met when I met John Booth was Marshall Brodein. Marshall was listed by *Magic* magazine as one of the 100 greatest magicians in history. He sold magic kits by infomercials in early television. He was Bozo the Clown on early TV.

He and his wife were backstage during a Lance Burton show. His wife wanted to write a book and I was the go-to guy for books at that time. I answered all her questions. I offered to help her. I didn't think anything of it. I was just being kind.

Marshall remembered it though.

He later sent me a box big enough to hold a small refrigerator. Inside were magic tricks. Maybe fifty or more. I was deliriously happy. I had collected magic tricks since I was a little kid; I bought them from mail order catalogs. Having this influential magician send me a huge box of magic was heart pounding. I smiled so big my face hurt for a week.

But Marshall's kindness didn't end there.

When he heard I was returning to Chicago some months later, he invited me to his home. I couldn't believe it. I couldn't say no.

He picked me up at my hotel, drove me to his home, and he and his wife fed me a glorious dinner. After, Marshall took me down to his basement, which he had turned into a magic museum and show room. He showed me around and explained the posters and props. He even performed magic for me. I stood there mouth gaping as he made a key vanish and appear later in his shoe. The guy was uncannily good.

I had questions about being nervous on stage.

"I was nervous the first few times," he said. "But practice gives you power and fearlessness."

I am grateful for Marshall and his unexpected kindness.

> "I expect to pass through life but once. If therefore, there be any kindness I can show, or any good thing I can do to any fellow being, let me do it now and not defer or neglect it, as I shall not pass this way again."
>
> —WILLIAM PENN

learned cooperation over competition when I needed to raise a lot of money fast and went to a copywriter in the same business as me.

David Garfinkel and I exchanged ideas, resources, leads, and more. We examined each other's sales letters. I never saw him as a competitor. He was my brother. We supported each other. So when I found a house I wanted to buy, when I didn't have the funds to buy it, I went to David.

"I need to raise about fifty grand," I told him. I just needed the down payment and moving funds.

David didn't bat an eye.

We kicked around ideas.

"You are such a big thinker and a bottomless pit of golden ideas," he said. "What if you took on a handful of clients for the year but insisted they pay for the year in advance?"

"Would anyone do that?"

"We won't know without trying."

We both knew trying and testing were how you found the secret to anything.

I wrote a sales letter that explained it all: why I needed the funds and why I was offering a discount. It was perfect "reason why" copywriting. David reviewed it, made some suggestions, and tweaked it.

I sent it out.

To my delight and amazement, people were overnighting cashier's checks for a year's fee to me. I raised over fifty grand in almost a single day.

I doubt I could have done it without David's unexpected kindness in brainstorming with me. I gave him a finder's fee percentage and was glad to do it. But the greater lesson is that I didn't need competitors when I had cooperation.

David and I are friends today, decades after his help, and support each other along life's journey.

> *Your acts of kindness are iridescent wings of divine love, which linger and continue to uplift others long after your sharing.*
>
> —RUMI

Around 1999, you couldn't enter a bookstore without seeing Bill Phillips' book on fitness or his magazine, *Muscle Media*. It seemed like he was the Alexander the Great of fitness, and was taking over the world, or at least the USA, with his challenge and mission.

The challenge was to get in shape in twelve weeks. The mission was to get people on board with fitness. Bill, his brother, and his company, seemed like a muscle-bound army of people trying to awaken the masses. I saw all of this and became mesmerized. I had been overweight virtually all my life. When I was about seventeen years old, I thought I would be heavyweight boxing champion of the world. I put myself through a workout program that was intense. I lost weight. I got fit. I was a force to reckon with. Even my father noticed. But I couldn't sustain it.

At some point I realized I would never be a great fighter. I didn't want to be punched in the face.

But the desire to be trim remained. When I saw the pages and pages of before and after photos in Bill's magazines, I stared in awe. Average people were transforming their bodies in the most dramatic ways. The people were real. The photos were real. The method was Bill's workout routines and his supplements. To make sure people got hooked on his dream, he offered cars to the top winners of the most impressive transformations.

Bill became a God to me. I went into his twelve-week program nine times. I kept quitting and starting again. Finally, I entered and stayed, and completed five contests. I lost eighty pounds in one year. I was committed. I was almost obsessed. I wanted to win. I had help from trainers.

Scott York continually performed unexpected kindness by driving down to my gym and training me. He checked in daily by email. He became my dearest friend and fitness buddy. I got an honorable mention for one contest. I still have the magazine listing all the winners, with my name in tiny type.

I met Bill briefly for the first time around 2007. We were both speaking at the same event in Austin. I stared at him as if he were otherworldly. He looked fit and very young. I looked and wondered, "Is that Bill or his son? He looks too young to be Bill."

I shyly made my way to him. I took a deep breath and extended my hand.

"Bill, my name is —"

"I know who you are, Joe."

"You do?"

"In LA we refer to the movie *The Secret* as the Michael and Joe show."

He was referring to Michael Beckwith, who's also in the movie.

"I was in your Body for Life program years ago," I said. "I lost eighty pounds."

"No way!" he exclaimed.

He was clearly and genuinely impressed.

I asked if I could have a photo with him. He agreed and I could see he was just as shy as I was. Neither of us were comfortable on stage. We could do it, but it took work.

It would be almost ten years before I saw Bill again.

I had gained weight. Lost weight. Gained it again. I still had my gym. I filled it with equipment that once belonged to legendary body builder Steve Reeves. Even famed actor and bodybuilder Lou Ferrigno came to see my gym. But I was frustrated at the constant battle to get and stay fit.

I looked Bill up. He was in Denver, running his own gym. He was now holding Transformation trainings. I called him.

"I want to see about being in the next training," I told the woman on the phone. She took my info and I signed up. But I wanted to ask for more.

"Is it possible to meet Bill and have lunch with him?"

I wasn't sure if a man so dedicated to fitness even ate lunch, but it was worth a shot. I wanted to meet the legend.

"I'm his wife," the woman said. "I'm sure I can arrange that."

She did. When I got to Denver and the gym, Bill made a fuss over me.

"I follow your work," he said. "You've really helped people with money issues and marketing."

I was flattered that this busy man knew my name at all. I stayed for the training and liked it so much I did it again and again. One of my lifetime achievements was finishing all the transformation contests and receiving medals from Bill for doing so. One of my cherished photos is Bill and I together, him handing me a medal.

Around 2009, I was hosting an event in Austin, Texas. I asked Bill if he would speak. I had no idea if would be insulted or flattered. Not only did he agree, but he waived his fee. He didn't want anything to appear on my stage. I was nearly in tears at his act of kindness and generosity. His speaking at my event is one of the highlights of my entire career.

In 2021, Bill asked me if I would help him write his new book. I quickly agreed. But before he could send me anything to review, he got seriously ill. It was either covid, or one of the viruses attached to it. He was in a coma. He lost seventy pounds of muscle. His wife sent out pleas to all friends, asking us to pray for him. He came around after a month, and slowly started to rebuild his body and his muscle.

I hadn't heard from Bill since his recovery until recently when he asked if I might help him with a new book on his health ordeal. I of course agreed. It'd be an honor. I'll always remember him and his loving acts of kindness.

> *"Too often we underestimate the power of a touch,*
> *a smile, a kind word, a listening ear, an honest*
> *compliment, or the smallest act of caring, all of*
> *which have the potential to turn a life around."*
>
> —LEO BUSCAGLIA

Another person I met during those struggle years when I taught adult education classes, was a young woman who later became one of the most powerful healing forces in my life.

Kathy Jo and I were attracted to each other. I felt it. I sensed she did. But I was in my first marriage and loyal to the bone. Still, I met with Kathy for coffee now and then, to discuss her writing goals, her life, and to follow our intuition.

We stayed in contact as life's currents swept us in different directions. When I started dating the woman who became my second wife, Kathy Jo helped protect me from my date's mother. Both my date and her mom were militant feminists who distrusted men. Her mother hated men. I feared for my life (literally) from her mom's wrath.

Kathy Jo had a sci-fi like intense power to throw a force field around me. She said she would keep me safe and she did. I had heard other stories of men who were attacked and shaken by the mom. A former Marine came to fix a windshield one day and the mom ripped him a new one. He came to the door, shaken. I felt his fear.

Kathy Jo performed her long-distance protection for me. Throughout my almost twenty years with my second wife, I was never harmed or even confronted by the mother. I truly feel Kathy Jo's esoteric work was the unexpected kindness that kept me safe.

As life moved on, my relationship with my second wife began to crumble. I filed for divorce. I offered my ex virtually everything to make life easier for her in this dramatic transition. She refused the easy way. I suffered a three-year persecution of my life and business. It was agonizing.

I went to Kathy Jo for help. She was there, again doing her magic from afar. As much as Kathy Jo worked, the drive, persecution, lawsuits, and pain continued. And during this same time, my father died, my best friend died, I developed a new relationship with a beautiful soul who attracted neuro-Lyme disease, and the pandemic hit.

Kathy Jo, even while having life issues of her own, was always there for me. I have never forgotten her and still stay in contact with her.

> *"Kindness is more important than wisdom, and the recognition of this is the beginning of wisdom."*
>
> —THEODORE RUBIN

isting the acts of kindness by Marc Gitterle would take a separate book. And I'm only talking about his kindness to me.

He's helped thousands of others, usually for no pay and no thanks. He wrote me around 2000, after reading my book *Spiritual Marketing*, before it was retitled *The Attractor Factor*. He shared that he sat beside the river in the woods, book in hand, and considered it devotional reading. When he noticed I lived in the same city as him, he reached out to me.

That was over twenty years ago. During the last two decades, he's become my medical doctor, spiritual advisor, sounding board, partner in alternative health products, confidant, ally, and dearest friend.

I don't know where to begin to acknowledge him.

Marc is a medical doctor. But he's far more than that. He's a scholar of alternative medicine and therapies. He got me into acupuncture. He is also deeply spiritual. He got me hiring Indian pundits to perform yagnas for me. When I went into the emergency room (ER) in Vegas, thinking I was having a heart attack, I contacted Marc. It turns out it was asthma and panic, but upon my return, I turned to Marc. He was there for me then and always.

When my first wife was taking dozens of prescription drugs, Marc reviewed the list and said, "This is a person who doesn't want to feel."

When I thought my stomach was going to explode, I called Marc and he calmly advised me to go to ER. There I was saved from an appendix that was about to burst. The doctor on call said I would have died had I not come in. Laying in bed in the hospital, Marc quietly came in and sat beside me, comforting me.

Whenever I had a health problem, I called Marc. He often drove right to my house, making a house call, virtually unheard of in these modern times. He saved me thousands of dollars in medical fees by advising me in person or on the phone.

When I had ideas for fitness and health products, I went to Marc. He became the medical authority for Fit-A-Rita, that healthy margarita mix I invented. The product never went anywhere, despite Whole Foods making an offer for thousands of packets, but Marc was always game to believe in me and my ideas, right down to putting his name on the label.

Having Marc in my life comforts me in a way difficult to describe. In the back of my mind, I know if I get ill, he's there. If I need a friend, he's there. If I have an idea for a product, he's there. When I heard all the advice he had for anti-aging, I urged him to write a book. He wrote *Growing Young*, which I still love today.

When I or my partner got ill, I'd contact Marc and he'd be there. I always marveled that he somehow found time to answer texts from me and others, while raising a family, running an emergency room, fielding calls from friends, and more. I've never known him not be there for me. It's beyond kindness. It's a benevolence of divine origin, coming through the man I know as Marc.

I met his mother at an event decades ago. When she said she was Marc's mother, I stared. I stared so long, without saying a word, that she looked nervous and said, "What's wrong?"

"I didn't know Marc had a mother," I said. "I assumed he was of divine origin, like Jesus."

> *"Kindness is more important than wisdom, and the recognition of this is the beginning of wisdom."*
> —THEODORE ISAAC RUBIN

My childhood desire to be the next Houdini never really left me. I spent a small fortune on magic, books, tricks, DVDs, and more. Every now and then I would incorporate a trick into my speaking gigs. But I really wanted to do something big.

When I met a magician who was also a corporate entertainer, we decided to host an event together. It became the world's first Spiritual Marketing Super Summit. I wanted to promote it in some sort of big, Barnum-like way. I had already booked a historic hotel in downtown Austin: the Driskill. It was said to be haunted. But I wanted more.

What about if I levitated in front of the hotel? It was on a busy main street in downtown Austin. I'd stop traffic. Surely people would take notice.

I had lived close to a famous magic bookstore when I lived in Houston. I asked the owner if he knew anyone who might help me perform magic. He did. And I ended up meeting a man who has shown nothing but unexpected kindness since the day we met, now decades ago. Kent Cummins and I corresponded at first. He was confused. He thought I was the famous sports announcer, Dick Vitale. I was often confused with the famous drummer, Joe Vitale (who in later years would become my drummer and dearest friend). I had to explain I was the marketing guy. Kent was into marketing, so we hit it off.

He spent a lot of time researching ways for me to levitate in public. Considering the average person who levitated was young and light, I'd probably not be able to get off the ground, no matter how much magic we applied. I was overweight. It might be better if I levitate someone else. We never did a levitation, but I was so grateful for Kent's help, that I gave him a ticket to my event. We've been friends ever since. In fact, when I decided to lighten my life's load and practice some unexpected giving, I gave Kent all my magic; the entire collection. There were boxes. He had to rent a U-Haul. I knew he would use it for the betterment of all local magicians.

> *"A single act of kindness throws out roots in all directions, and the roots spring up and make new trees."*
> —AMELIA EARHART

My first wife died in 2005. We were divorced in 1999, but remained best friends till the end. I spoke to her or wrote to her every day. I loved her. She was fun and funny, sensitive and stirring, loving and supportive. She supported me when I was an unemployed struggling writer. We both loved animals and raised our cats from feral babies born next door to us. Losing her caused me to fold over in pain. I cried every day for a year.

Joe Sugarman heard of my grief. Joe is a legendary marketer; one of the true icons of copywriting and direct mail. He was a big thinker and outrageous advertiser. He made a fortune from selling BluBlocker sunglasses by infomercial. He bought up properties on Maui when they were affordable, at least to the moderately wealthy. When Joe heard of my first wife's death, he invited me and my new partner to come to Hawaii and stay as his guests in one of his Maui beach front homes.

Joe was wonderful. He liked and respected me. He put us up in a home that was mega glorious. Stephen Tyler and the entire Aerosmith band had stayed in the house right before us. Joe introduced us to alternative healers. He was publishing a local newspaper at the time and knew everyone. He introduced us to many influencers, including politicians, real estate brokers, big and small businesspeople, and more.

Joe spoke at one of my events. He didn't charge me anything. He was riveting, telling stories about trying to sell Batman credit cards, his work in infomercials, and more. Everyone loved him. He was funny and wise.

One day as we were driving around Maui, he offered an observation.

"You have two traits of the three needed for great power," he once told me.

"What do you mean?"

"You are a great orator," he began. "Speaking ability is one of the ways to gain power in the world."

"I do?" I questioned, demonstrating my lack of speaking skills.

"You have the gift of gab," he said.

He had my attention.

"You are also a great writer," he said. "Being able to write is one of the most powerful ways to move the masses. You have that gift."

"And the third?"

"Great wealth," he said.

"I'm working on that one," I said.

"Two out of three is rare," Joe explained. "You can move the world with writing and speaking skills, and you're working on having great wealth. You are positioned with enough skills to rule any area you want to rule."

He said that around 2005 and I'm still processing it today. Joe Sugarman's unexpected kindness was unforgettable.

Unfortunately, as I was writing these words, I learned Joe passed away. I am shaken and sad, but also grateful that such a legendary, colorful, amazing genius took time to befriend, encourage, and inspire me.

> *"Kindness doesn't cost a thing."*
>
> —RUSSELL BRUNSON

Actor James Caan called me as I drove to my first wife's funeral.

His trainer was a remarkably kind man who came to me for marketing advice. During the opening of our relationship, he learned my first wife had passed. As I shared, she and I remained best friends after our divorce. Her death shattered my world.

TR Goodman had a lot of celebrity clients, most of them tough guys like Ray Liotta and James Caan. He said he would have James call me.

He did.

"Joe? It's Jimmie."

James Caan liked people to call him Jimmie. I couldn't do it.

The star of *The Godfather* and dozens of other films was on a pedestal in my world. I could barely stammer the stupid line, "It's an honor to talk to you."

Jimmie didn't respond to my flattery. He probably saw it as BS. He was a tough, no-nonsense guy.

So, I repeated it.

"It's an honor to meet you." Dead silence.

"What are you doing?" he asked.

"I'm in a car on my way to a funeral."

"A funeral? What the hell? Who died?"

"My ex."

"Your ex? Your ex died?" he repeated. "I'm sorry for your loss, but I'm glad it was your ex. I have a lot of exes I'd like to see trade places with yours."

I laughed. It was James Caan humor. I was floored that this stunning legendary actor was reaching out to me.

"Do you have any advice for me?" I asked.

I figured he'd been married multiple times, was older than me, and maybe had some wisdom to share.

"Advice? You want advice from me?" he said, repeating everything I said. "You don't want advice from me, Joe. I haven't got this marriage thing right yet."

I laughed. I was grieving but everything he said sounded funny.

"He's laughing," Jimmie told somebody in the room.

"I'm a huge fan," I said.

"You take care," he said. "Come see me when you come out here. Talk to you later."

At the funeral, when I got up to speak, I told everyone about James Caan calling me.

My late ex-wife idolized Caan, loved movies, and repeatedly watched *The Godfather*. She would have loved the fact that Jimmie and I talked.

Months later I did fly out to LA to meet the trainer and talk business. We went to the gym many of the stars train at in Santa Monica. I met Ray Liotta. I also met Jimmie.

"What the hell you doing here?" he asked.

"You said we'd talk later," I said. "Well, it's later."

Jimmie was super cool and super kind.

We went to the set where he was starring in the TV series *Las Vegas*. I was shocked to see it was a rundown building with rotting floorboards.

We got on a golf cart and he drove me around. I sat beside him on the cart, asking questions that felt stupid.

"The hamburger they fed you in one episode, was that really cooked by a famous chef?"

"They probably said it was but it was a cold piece of meat, just a prop for the show."

But he was patient.

"Our writers need your help," he told me. "Their scripts suck. They write with crayons."

"I'll help if I can," I said, feebly, as I didn't realize Jimmie was just being nice. His show was a hit. His writers were great.

"Thanks for the tour," I told him.

"All I ask is you take care of TR," he said.

James Caan was being kind to me, hoping that I would be kind to his trainer and friend. It was the full circle of unexpected kindness.

They were both involved in a mixed martial arts contest they wanted to promote. TR showed me the promotion film.

"Joe, what did you think?" Jimmie asked me.

"It wasn't that great," I said, fearing being honest might get me killed, but knowing I had to flaunt my marketing expertise.

"Why's that?" Jimmy asked.

"Your part in the film was stellar," I told Jimmy. "But the promo begins with data and it needs to begin with emotion. I'd put your part up front."

"Let's do that then," he told TR.

I don't know if they ever edited the film or not, but Jimmie made me feel great because he asked for and listened to my opinions.

I loved his raw humor. I asked for an autographed photo.

"You gay or what?" he asked.

"I'm a fan," I said.

His assistant handed Jimmie a photo. Jimmie was about to sign it when he looked at me.

"Can I write anything?" he asked.

"You're James Caan," I replied. "Write whatever you want."

He scribbled something on the photo and called TR over. "Look what I wrote," he said.

TR laughed.

I looked. The signature said: "To Joe, you are a big pain in the ass."

He signed it, too.

I loved it and still have it.

When I left him and stepped outside, I was standing face to face to one of the most beautiful cars I had ever seen.

"What's this car?" I asked TR.

"That's Jimmie's car."

"It is? I want it."

"It's a Bentley," TR told me. "When Jimmie goes to sell it, I'll have him call you."

He kept his word.

Months later James Caan and I spoke on the phone about his Bentley. "I love it," he said. "But it's a temporary car while they make a Bentley for me. My custom one is done and this one is ready to be returned to the dealer or sold."

I was interested but it'd be the most expensive car of my life.

"Come on out to my house and I'll let you drive it," he said. "One of my writers wants it, but TR said you spoke up first. I don't need to make anything on it. I'll sell it for what I paid."

Ultimately, I passed. A luxury car of that price wasn't in my self-image yet. It would be another ten years before I could comfortably afford and enjoy my own Bentley. By then Jimmie's was sold and history.

As I was writing this, Jimmy died. It crushed me. I had hoped to see him again. The pandemic was keeping me home, and I wasn't seeing anyone. But I was in tears when I learned of his death, and almost cry daily even now. He was known as a tough guy, and he was, but he was good to me.

I never forgot the actor's unexpected kindness to me.

> *"Kindness is like snow—*
> *It beautifies everything it covers."*
> —KAHLIL GIBRAN

An email can change a life.

I still remember the email that shocked me in 2005.

I was headed to Rome with my second wife. I would be the first in my family to go to Italy since my grandparents immigrated to the USA around 1915. I was excited and told my email list, which was about 800 names or less back then.

Somebody on the list wrote back with a thunderbolt.

"I see you are coming to Rome. If you would like to meet the Pope, I can arrange it. I am the nun serving him."

I didn't believe it at first.

How could anyone on my list know anyone at the Vatican?

And the Pope at that time was the beloved Pope John Paul.

Somebody on my list knew HIM?

I was yet to learn how connected the world really is, especially thanks to the internet. I wrote back and wrote something flippant but polite.

"Sure, I'll meet the Pope, if he has nothing else to do one day."

I forgot about it, packed, and boarded the flights overseas. When we landed and I found a way to check email (before the iPhone, remember?). I saw that the nun was inviting me to visit the Vatican and where the nuns who serve the pope stay. She said she would pick us up at our hotel.

She did.

Sister Mary Elizabeth was a jittery little woman from New Jersey. Her devotion and passion for the church moved her up the ranks. She was serving Pope John Paul, bringing him lasagna on Wednesdays.

"I'm going to get your book to the pope," she told me.

Back then she was referring to *Spiritual Marketing*, which later became my bestseller *The Attractor Factor.* But at that point in time, we were years away from *The Secret* or any world fame.

Yet my internet success was getting noticed.

"Having you here is like having Mickey Mantle visit," she said.

Not everyone remembers the legendary baseball player. I did and knew it was a compliment. I was a celebrity to Sister.

"We used your hypnotic writing methods to raise funds," she told me.

Hypnotic Writing was my first eBook. I had no idea the Catholic church knew of it.

"We used the methods in your book and rewrote our fund-raising letters," she explained. "As a result, we raised far more funds. Hypnotic writing really works."

"What did you do different?" I asked.

"Little things like telling a story," she explained, "and adding a PS. Your ideas really helped us."

She gave us a tour of Rome, took us to Vatican City, and brought us to where the nuns stay who serve the high priests of the Vatican.

She sat us down and fed us a nine-course meal. They were small portions, much the size of tapas that I would discover decades later in Spain.

They made wine and lemon cello right there at the nuns' home. They gave us bottles of each.

While I had been disappointed that no relatives turned out to greet my arrival, I've never forgotten the unexpected kindness of Sister Mary Elizabeth and the nuns at the Vatican.

I never did meet the pope in person, but I had a private audience with him. Private if you count two hundred souls in the same area.

It was in the outdoor area of the Vatican.

He spoke to all of us in different languages. I still remember my awe at hearing him speak in English. He spoke more perfectly than me.

Later I learned Pope John Paul did receive a copy of my book *Spiritual Marketing*.

One of the nuns put it under his lasagna tray on Wednesday and delivered both. I never heard whether he read the book or liked it, but it's a warm thought to imagine him thumbing through it, smiling, as he ate lasagna.

> *"Kindness in words creates confidence.*
> *Kindness in thinking creates profoundness.*
> *Kindness in giving creates love."*
> —LAO TZU

While in Italy visiting Florence, the tour guide led us to a leather shop. I saw some of the most beautiful, softest, luxurious coats and accessories. I had never seen such craftsmanship. I was in awe of the quality. No wonder Italian leather goods were so popular worldwide.

I pulled a leather shirt off a rack. It was super soft, smooth, light, and oh-so comfortable. It was suede and light brown.

It felt glorious on me. I wanted to strut and swagger. I showed my wife.

"I don't like it," she said.

My spirit dropped. I was hurt. I loved the feel of the shirt. "It doesn't look good on you," she added.

It felt good. I thought it looked good. But if my wife was going to look at me with disgust whenever I wore it, I'd never be able to wear it.

Regrettably, I hung the leather shirt-jacket back up. But I never forgot it.

I remembered it on our trip back from Italy.

I remembered it whenever I looked in my closet.

I remembered it whenever I lay in bed and couldn't sleep.

Years went by. I attended a marketing seminar in Vegas. My publisher was there. I met Jack Canfield for the first time there. And I spoke to the group about sales and marketing.

Two men came up to me afterwards. It was clear they were from Italy. "Where are you from?" I asked.

"Florence."

Florence!

Suddenly images of the leather shirt I left behind started flashing into my mind. I told the gentlemen all about the experience; how I regretted leaving the shirt.

"Do you remember the store you saw it in or the brand?"

I did. I had kept the business card from the store.

"Send us the info," one of the Italians said.

Later, I did.

A few weeks went by and suddenly my personal assistant was calling me.

"There are two guys on the phone saying they are in Florence, Italy, and need to know your jacket size."

I was stunned. I knew it was the gentlemen I met in Vegas. They went back home, went to the leather store, and were looking for the jacket, or one like it, that I left behind.

"They told me to go in your closet and check your size," my assistant laughed.

It was funny considering she worked in her office and I in mine and we almost never visited or saw each other.

In short, the two gentlemen went back to their home in Florence, went to the store I told them about, and bought me the leather jacket I left behind. They shipped it to me. Not only that, they shipped two jackets to me, in case one didn't fit or was the wrong color.

The jacket fit.

It was exactly like the one I left behind.

The gents sent it as a gift.

It was an unexpected kindness that I still wear today.

> *"Kindness is the language which the deaf can hear and the blind can see."*
>
> —MARK TWAIN

What would you say if I gave you a choice of three items to have as a gift?"

I was walking around the trade show floor at a new age convention with Lori Anderson. She was a fan who became a friend. Over ten years, we became supporters and confidantes of each other. She had just heard me speak and was asking me a tough question.

"What?"

"I know you want the handmade drum, and the painting we saw, and the gemstone stand," she explained. "I'd like to buy one of them for you. Which do you want most?"

I stared at her.

I felt myself sweat.

I knew Lori had just begun a divorce and her funds were shrinking. I also knew I had just talked about the power of giving to my audience, and Lori was in the crowd. She was practicing giving.

But could I practice receiving?

That's when I really felt the difficulty in accepting gifts. All the limiting beliefs about deservingness flashed through my mind. I had to remind myself that not accepting a gift was interrupting my own flow of prosperity. Money has to circulate. Plus I knew depriving Lori of what she wanted to do from the goodness of her heart was also hurting her.

"The drum," I finally answered.

"Let's go get it," she said.

When we arrived at the booth for the Native American wood worker, we saw a man in desperate need of a sale. His drum was astonishingly beautiful, hand carved with polished wood and a genuine deer skin top. It was a work of art. But there was no one buying anything that we could see.

"I'd like to buy that drum for Joe," Lori said.

The young man with the handmade vest and gentle spirit smiled and picked it up. The tag on it said the price.

One thousand dollars.

"Are you sure?" I asked Lori.

"Absolutely, yes!" she said, beaming.

I still have the drum today, almost fifteen years after Lori bought it for me.

What neither Lori nor I knew at the time was the craftsman who made the drum was broke. He couldn't pay any of his bills. He didn't have gas money to get home. The $1,000 saved the day and probably his life, at least as he saw it.

So I got a drum.

The builder got the money.

And Lori felt the joy of giving.

But her unexpected kindness doesn't end there. It triggered wins for everyone involved in the transaction.

The woodworker became one of my friends and clients. I later invested in his new, fledgling company. I hired him to make several leather vests for me.

Lori became one of my closest and longest friends. I helped her write her book, *Divorce with Grace*. We met almost monthly for years to brainstorm ideas and support each other. When she went through a long, ugly divorce, I was there for her. When I went through my own divorce, Lori was there for me.

While the pandemic prevented our regular meetings, we still stay in contact. She became friends with my love, Lisa Winston.

All from the unexpected kindness of giving me a drum.

> *"Kindness gives birth to kindness."*
>
> —SOPHOCLES

was still answering my phone back in 2005, so it wasn't unusual for a strange woman calling from Australia to reach me. But what was unusual was her request.

It turns out she was a TV producer in Melbourne. I love the city and told her so. We chatted a bit about Australia before she got to the point.

"I'm going to make a movie about the Law of Attraction," she began. "I want you in it."

"I've never been in a movie, and why me?"

"I read your book *The Attractor Factor*," she said. "I loved it. You would be perfect for the film."

I didn't know what to believe. But I didn't believe her. At that point, I had heard from dozens of people who said they were going to write a book or open a business and simply disappeared. They did nothing. I assumed this woman was just blowing smoke.

"I can send you the trailer I made to promote the movie," she said. "Don't share it, but it will give you a good feel for what I want to do."

I told her I would take a look. She emailed the movie preview. I watched it.

I was fried.

It was only a minute or two long, but was so dramatic, rousing, theatrical, and epic that I felt like I had been hit by lightning. The movie trailer was a masterpiece.

I instantly wrote her.

"I want in," I said. "If your movie is anything like the trailer, it will be unforgettably great."

Little did I know at the time that she had already filmed about sixty people for the movie. She went to one of the meetings of the Transformational Leadership Council, this one in Denver, and filmed every single person there. They were all thought leaders, speakers, authors, consultants, and authorities.

But I wasn't a member of the group (not then, I am now) and I wasn't at that meeting. That meant Rhonda went out of her way to contact me. It was an unexpected kindness that would alter the course of my life.

She flew me to Chicago, filmed me for two hours, and sent me back home to Texas.

She told me "The camera loves you, Joe."

I figured she said that to all her guests. Out of the twenty-four teachers in the movie, I am one of the five most people think of when they talk about *The Secret*. I credit that as an unexpected kindness from the universe.

As you can probably guess, being in *The Secret* catapulted me into a whole new world of opportunities, publicity, media, deals, and attention. The movie is still being seen in countries around the world. While I and the others in the movie were never paid, nor received any compensation, I for one never complained. I would endorse that movie whether I was in it or not. I'm grateful for being in it.

It's an unexpected kindness that blesses in the most benevolent way.

> *"Kindness is more than deeds.*
> *It is an attitude, an expression, a look, a touch.*
> *It is anything that lifts another person."*
>
> —PLATO

Dr. Hew Len didn't know me when I called him in 2005. I heard the wild story of a therapist who helped heal an entire ward of mentally-ill criminals by working on himself. It made no sense. I wanted to know the story. I searched. I hired a private investigator. I found the therapist. And I called him.

He spent forty-five minutes on the phone with me. It was an act of kindness and generosity as he didn't know me. I was sincere. I was curious. And I was so taken by the man's story and energy that I decided to fly to California and meet him.

I liked him instantly. He had a soft, relaxed, gentle way about him. He seemed to like me and spent time talking to me during breaks at the first seminar I attended with him. Back then, few knew him or his work, so the event barely had twenty people in the room. What he spoke of didn't always make sense, but I felt he was speaking from beyond 3-D reality. He was the teacher, and I was the student, eager to learn.

It was a plot twist in my life. Dr. Hew Len was like an odd grandfather; a mystic with a twisted sense of humor and a confusing method of healing. I wanted to know more. I ended up hosting three events with him, writing the first book to bring his method to the masses with his guidance, and having my life changed forever. He named me "Ao Akua," which he explained meant "parting the clouds to see God."

He taught me modern ho'oponopono. It was and is a simple way to transform yourself by saying four phrases: I love you, I'm sorry, please forgive me, and thank you. There is plenty of depth in those phrases, which I've shared in my books, *Zero Limits*, *At Zero*, and *The Fifth Phrase*.

Dr. Hew Len passed away in January 2022. I remember him being kind, patient, and understanding, at least with me. I saw him gruff and snappy with others. He didn't want to speak or travel. He wanted to tend to his garden. He was getting older. But the Divine, he would say, kept urging him out the door. In 2022, it all ended.

I have fond memories of him. I will be forever grateful for his unexpected kindness.

> *"What wisdom can you find that*
> *is greater than kindness?"*
> —JEAN-JACQUES ROUSSEAU

The comet in my life hit in 2006.

Once the movie *The Secret* was released, the world took notice of me. I went on Larry King's TV show twice. Oprah's people called, inviting me to be on her show. Hollywood wanted me to have my own talk show.

Book deals came in and speaking engagements were offered. More movies were being made and wanting me in them. Overseas events blossomed and wanted me at them.

It was a whirlwind of activity for the next fifteen years, and it hasn't really stopped, despite a pandemic, time, and world events.

Old friends who disappeared over time resurfaced. People I worked for or with showed up. Everyone was kind, but not unexpectedly so. They saw me as a celebrity of sorts and wanted to be near the flame. I made new friends of course, developed new partners, and created new courses, books, audios, events, and more.

There were a few standout people during those exhilarating years.

One of them was an inventor who developed a type of artificial intelligence boxing machine. It had a computer screen that showed a boxer taking jabs. It had pads with electrodes in them, so when you hit it, it took count. It was called a Nexersys.

I loved it.

It brought back my childhood dreams of being a boxer. The difference is, when I hit the Nexersys, it didn't hit back.

Terry Jones gave me one. I had my own gym at the time. It was filled with equipment that had been used by Steve Reeves, the actor and famous body builder from the golden age. Whenever my trainer came to see me, we used it. Scott York was another unexpectedly kind soul during those times. He would drive over an hour each way to visit me, train me, and encourage me.

When I filed for divorce, I started giving away collections. I gave all of my Reeve's collection to Scott York. He had been kind to me. He never charged me for all that training. I wanted to give back. I already mentioned giving my magic collection to Kent Cummins. I gave boxes of books to Chuck Pennington, my friend and tech guy for over ten years.

Along the way, Terry checked in.

I told him I was in the midst of a divorce, now living in an apartment, and had given away the Nexersys. I told him of my struggles and stresses.

"Sounds like you need another machine," he said.

He then arranged for me to receive a second Nexersys.
I was speechless. In awe of his generosity.

Months passed and I had lunch with him. I was researching for my book, *Karmic Marketing*, and wanted him in it.

"Why did you give me two machines?"

"It feels great to give."

During our conversation, I told him of my client in Thailand who had a gym. Andres Pira was the once homeless now billionaire who said he owed his success to me, Bob Proctor, and Jack Canfield.

"Get me his address and I'll ship one to him, too."

Terry's unexpected kindness was off the charts. I still have the second Nexersys. And my friend in Thailand still has his.

> "We cannot tell the precise moment when friendship is formed. As in filling a vessel drop by drop, there is at last a drop which makes it run over; so in a series of kindnesses there is at last one which makes the heart run over."
>
> —RAY BRADBURY

I never wanted to go to Poland.

Ever.

All I remembered were the Polish jokes I heard growing up.

So, when I received an invite to speak in Poland, I inflated my rates so the agent would balk and say no thanks. But he agreed. So I asked for more, like a box of Cuban cigars, a bottle of rare Scotch, etc. The agent agreed to all of it. Shoot. I had to go to Poland.

My wife at the time was more interested than me. She played Polish language tapes on the trip over. I slept or watched movies. After the long flight there, we landed and met our agent and guide. From that moment on, unexpected kindness was the norm.

Andriez took pains to be sure we were happy. He knew I drove a BMW at the time, so he rented a BMW. He knew I liked good food, so he took us out for an amazing dinner. He knew our luggage had been lost in transit, so he took us out to get new clothes. He gave me cigars, Scotch, and a tour of the city of Warsaw. He made sure both of us were treated like royalty.

I so loved Andriez and our time in Poland that we went back four times. I felt true love for the man. He was funny and smart and consistently caring. I'm sorry to say he passed away. I felt his loss like I would a brother. He was a rare gem. And he practiced unexpected kindness as others practiced breathing.

> *"Three things in human life are important.*
> *The first is to be kind.*
> *The second is to be kind.*
> *And the third is to be kind."*
>
> —HENRY JAMES

My first trip to Russia was no picnic.

I grew up hearing Russia was the enemy. They could bomb us without notice. We practiced air raids in school, crawling under our wooden desks for cover. So when I was invited to travel to Russia and speak there, I didn't want to go. Childhood fears remained in my adult body.

But I went.

The people who hired me to come to their country had never put on events before. I didn't know that. My team didn't know that. It wasn't until I traveled for fourteen hours or more and landed in Moscow that I discovered what was expected of me.

A lot.

I was barely off the plane and in their car when they said they were taking me to an interview. Right then. I was stunned. My chest dropped. I was speechless and couldn't believe it. No time for a shower? A change of clothes? A little rest before activities began?

Nope.

But I had traveled, and I was there, so I bit my tongue and did what was asked.

The pace never let up anywhere: from Moscow to St. Petersburg to Siberia, and notably the city of Novosibirsk. Throughout it all I would playfully ask where the Russian guitars were. I loved music and wanted to add a Russian guitar to my growing collection. But no one could tell me anything. Or show me anything.

Until I was on stage in Siberia. The people there were warm and friendly, in a country that was cold and scary. But I was on stage when the promoter of that leg of the campaign walked in with an acoustic guitar. It was a seven string Russian instrument. He walked right up to the stage and handed it to me in front of everyone. It was like a dream. Even I was speechless. I had been asking to see one, and here one was given to me.

"This is how it works," I told the audience. "You ask and you let go and what you want comes to you."

I was oversimplifying, of course. I asked and continued to ask.

Surprisingly, considering how difficult it was to leave Russia in a hurry, the guitar made it all the way back to Texas with me. I still have it. It's a reminder of the benevolence of a people I once feared.

While the country remains a threat, millions of people within it are like you and me, regular people wanting to live happy lives, and often practicing unexpected kindness.

> "Human kindness has never weakened the
> stamina or softened the fiber of a free people."
> —FRANKLIN D. ROOSEVELT

wasn't going to write about Mathew Dixon. He saw
The Secret in a movie premiere at a Unity Church that I
arranged and spoke at circa 2005. He wrote to me and
asked to meet. I figured he was being kind because he
knew me from the movie. He was.

But he didn't know I wanted to learn how to play guitar. He was a neo-flamingo player and teacher. He gave
me his CD. I wrote to him. We met and I hired him to
teach me guitar at my home.

Being shrewd and wise, he made me an offer:

"I'll come to your home and teach you guitar for forty-
five minutes, and you answer my questions about internet
marketing for fifteen minutes, and we'll call it even."

I loved helping people with ideas and online com-
merce. And I wanted to play guitar. I agreed.

Mathew started coming over weekly. I paid him at
first, though that wasn't the agreement. I just slipped
him a hundred for each session. It was Karmic Market-

ing or tithing, depending on your view. But over time, we developed products and albums together. He attended my Zero Limits events, played guitar over lunch, met Dr. Hew Len, and became a dear friend.

We both went through a divorce. We both went through the pandemic. We both struggled in our own ways with the earthquakes of life. I didn't see much of him during those years. But one day Mathew did something so unexpectedly kind that it brought me to instant tears.

"I have something for you," he told me over the phone. "Can you meet me at the front door?"

When he pulled in the driveway, I opened the door. He unloaded a huge box. I guessed it was probably a musical instrument, but I didn't know what. I also noticed he was shaking.

"I can't stay," he said, stuttering and visibly shaking. "I've never done anything like this. This is the biggest thing I've ever done."

I felt his nervousness. I assured him he was fine to leave. I'd take the box inside and call him later.

I laid the box on our ping pong table. Then I unlatched all the holders and opened it.

I gasped.

Tears came to my eyes.

I was shaken.

I knew what it took for Mathew to give me this gift. He still lived just above poverty. He still struggled. He still fought with lack and limitation. Yet he gave me one of the greatest gifts of my life.

It was a handmade V-shaped electric guitar, made by one of the most notable guitar makers in the country, Tony Nobles. I had seen pics of the guitar. Despite my struggling with a divorce at the time, I had offered to buy it from Nobles. But he said, "Joe Walsh wants it." I shrugged and figured Joe could use it more than me.

But I never forgot the guitar.

It was made out of rare wood, hand carved over months, and shone like a museum piece. I also knew it cost around $5,000. Maybe more.

Tony Nobles described his guitar this way:

I always liked Lonnie Mack's V with the Bigsby. I made the V from Black Limba, what Gibson calls Korina. It is light and very resonant. The fingerboard is old Brazilian rosewood, all the shell inlay is mother of pearl. The inlay in the back of the headstock was inspired by a Gibson Super 400. The binding is laminated grained ivoroid made from celluloid. The headstock overlay is ebony. There are carbon fiber rods in the neck as well as the adjustable truss rod. I made the bigsby bracket from billet aluminum. The pickups are Gibson Burst Bucker plus, the electronic components are from The Art of Tone with Orange drop tone caps. The tuners are Grover Imperials. The finish is nitrocellulose lacquer, hand rubbed. I basically built it like a Gibson from the 50s with the addition of the carbon fiber which makes it even better.

And Mathew bought it and gave it to me.
I called him.

"Mathew, I am shaking. I opened it and tears burst. I know the value and I know the gift. I know how hard it was for you to give this to me."

"Well, don't tell anyone I gave it to you. I wanted to give it anonymously but none of our mutual friends would agree to do it. They told me to do it."

During a brief meeting over a cigar in 2021, I asked Mathew if I could share the story of the guitar he gave me. He agreed. He sensed it might inspire others to practice uncomfortable giving.

It was an act of unexpected kindness, and the guitar sits right beside me. You can see it on almost every video I make.

> *"In nothing do men more nearly approach the gods than by doing good to their fellow man."*
>
> —CICERO

Speaking of guitars.

I wasn't going to include this story but it's too good to pass up.

In 2014, I received a mega gift in Las Vegas—a late sixtieth birthday present—that was so unexpected, overwhelming, rare, loving, priceless, and magnificent, that I'm still nearly speechless. Most of the following is from my 2014 blog post about the unexpected kindness.

Over fifty people were involved—none were paid, all gave out of love and generosity—and the result was a gift of such magnitude and historic importance that I'm not sure how to describe it.

But here goes . . .

I love everyone in my Miracles Coaching program. The coaches and staff are upbeat, positive, loving, and loveable people.

Once a year the top coaches and salespeople meet me in Las Vegas for a dinner, awards ceremony, sharing, meeting, and more. I always look forward to the trips and the catching up.

Over this dinner, they hinted early on that they had a surprise for me. I figured it'd be a cigar or a book. I didn't think too much of it. I wasn't there for me. I was there for them. Little did I know that their little surprise would change my life forever.

Steve Gardner, one of the team leaders, began.

He handed me a little key.

I joked that it must be for a little car.

Wrong.

Turns out it was to a guitar case.

Not to any guitar, though.

What these people had done was build the world's first Clearing Guitar.

It was hand crafted out of Kauri wood estimated to be over 50,000 years old, and included gems in the fret board, and other healing mojo to make it a truly one-of-a-kind healing guitar. It was crafted of other wood that I love, such as koa, flame maple, and purple heart. It contains unique additions, such as a mammoth tooth estimated to be over 12,000 years old. It also has chakra stones for fret markers, and more.

It's tuned to the 424 Hz frequency, said to be more harmonious to our bodies than the standard 440 Hz.

And it is a baritone electric guitar.

I'm still in awe of this incredible, personalized guitar with such healing qualities, made with such precision and care.

I've never seen anything like it.

More than that, they built it *for me*.

They talked to Guitar Monk Mathew Dixon, my guitar teacher and partner on several instrumental musical albums, to determine what kind of guitar would be best for me. He told them of my love for baritones.

With the inside information from Mathew, and further insights about clearing and ho'oponopono from Suzanne Burns, my right (and left) hand partner in business at the time, they went to work.

The whole idea was the brainchild of Abi White. She went to her friend, luthier Mark Seddon of Oxbow Guitars in the U.K., and they began the process.

In the end, six months later, over fifty people gave products or services to help create this Miracle Guitar that they call The Clearing Guitar.

Mark named it Morrnah, after Morrnah Simeona, who gave us all modern ho'oponopono (as described in my books, *At Zero*, *Zero Limits*, and *The Fifth Phrase*).

They presented the guitar to me in Las Vegas.

After I heard the story of its creation, I was almost speechless.

When I held the guitar, I felt the love.

When I played it, I felt the magic.

But the story gets even better.

Abi, who came up with the idea, and Mark, the luthier who crafted the guitar, flew to Vegas from London to meet me the next morning.

Mark answered my questions about the guitar and set it up for me to play for everyone at our private meeting in Vegas.

It was a joyful experience to strum such a one-of-a-kind baritone electric guitar, with the unusual but soothing 424 Hz frequency tuning, and all the esoteric specifics that went into it, as everyone involved in Miracles Coaching watched and applauded.

Abi White summed up the creation of this guitar this way . . .

"For me this guitar inspired by Joe and manifest through myself, the team at Achieve Today, Mat Dixon, Mark Seddon, and so many others whom I love and am very grateful for, is far more than just a guitar. It is a stunning, beautiful, completely balanced, highly powerful clearing tool that I hope will assist and support Joe in the work he is doing in the world to bring healing and clearing through music, or as Mat Dixon The Guitar Monk puts it far more eloquently: 'To simply call this a guitar would be an understatement; it is a Masterpiece! A one-of-a-kind piece of art, created with love by all those involved.'"

And for me . . .

It's difficult to describe the love and gratitude I feel.

When I realize that fifty some people were feeling such love and gratitude for me, that they wanted to create this for me, the feeling of love is almost incomprehensible.

The morning after my receiving the guitar, I walked out of The Venetian luxury hotel, guitar in hand, and stepped up to the waiting limousine.

People stared. They probably wondered if I were a rock star of some sort who just played Vegas the night before.

Well, I *had* played Vegas the night before. It was in a small room, to some of the most angelic and loving people I've ever known.

Talk about an unexpected kindness and an unforgettable memory.

held a small autograph party in an upstairs area of a local restaurant circa 2005. It was a small town. I mentioned the event in my email to my list, which went to people worldwide. It was not likely that anybody would be living nearby.

I was wrong.

A young woman with lots of questions came. She was on my mailing list. She lived a few miles away. She wanted to meet me and ask questions about online marketing. She was a singer. We had a nice chat and then she left. I figured she'd never return.

But she came back a few minutes later, carrying a guitar.

"What's up?" I asked.

"I want to play a song for you."

I didn't know at the time but later learned she was terrified. She felt like her legs were made of concrete as she climbed the stairs. This was a huge moment for her, and for me.

"Everyone, can you stop a minute?!" I said to the group.

Everyone kept talking.

I turned to one of the big burly guys with a baritone voice and asked him to quiet the group.

"QUIET!" he bellowed.

The room went dead silent.

"Sarah here wants to sing a song."

The young woman then fried us all by singing an operatic aria.

Everyone was in awe.

I had expected a John Denver folk song, not some Italian riff that gave me goosebumps.

We became friends.

We talked music, life, goals, and dreams. She created a ho'oponopono inspired album of music and I paid to help her produce it. When I recorded my first album, Blue Healer, Sarah appeared on it.

Years later, Sarah McSweeney was my music mentor when I got ready to perform on stage with my Band of Legends. I was terrified and told her so. She supported me, encouraged me, and was in the audience of the show. I got a standing ovation. Sarah was there standing too.

And when I performed solo, without my band, at my love Lisa's "Own the Stage" event, Sarah was there. I kept talking on stage, delaying the moment when I would pick up my guitar and sing, but the moment came. Sarah had someplace to go, as she told me earlier, but she stayed to see my moment on stage.

But her unexpected kindness wasn't all the musical encouragement. It was on one of my birthdays. I always complained about my birthday being four days after Christmas and people forgetting it. Sarah did something about it.

"I have a surprise for you," she said.

She picked me up and drove me off. We went up and down back roads outside of Wimberley, Texas. I had already lived in the area almost twenty years but had no clue where she was taking me.

"Is there a motel out here?" I flirted. "A secret cabin?" She just smiled.

After what seemed like an especially long drive to nowhere, she pulled up at some ranch house hidden in the woods. She had to enter a code to unlock a gate. Then we had to drive even further.

Where was she taking me?

It turned out to be the home of a man who built guitars. Sarah knew of my love for the instrument. She also knew this luthier was unknown to me.

The jolly fellow who came out gave me a tour of his workshop. He was new to guitar making but had some impressive acoustics. Sarah had bought one from him and loved it.

"How did you learn how to build guitars?"

"From books," he replied.

I loved the guy right there. Books are my passion and purpose, my friends, and advisers. Knowing another soul learned his craft from books warmed my heart.

On another birthday, she presented me with a song she wrote just for me. She performed it for me in private, recorded it, gave me the track, and made sure my birthday was unforgettable.

Sarah's unexpected kindness became golden memories for me.

> *"Kind words do not cost much.*
> *Yet they accomplish much."*
>
> —BLAISE PASCAL

went to Sarah when a guitar maker in Canada wanted to give one of his guitars away.

Dimitry was from Russia, but moved to Canada. Though he had been an engineer, he started building guitars. They were unique and memorable. I had already bought three from him. But he had built one he didn't want to sell.

"I want it to go to some child who wants to play," he explained. "I don't know how to reach kids, but you probably do."

I didn't, but Sarah did. Most of her students were teenagers. So I asked her if she knew one who would welcome a new guitar valued at over five thousand dollars.

She did.

We arranged for Sarah and the youth to come to my house. His name was Loki. We presented the acoustic guitar to him. He was already shy and uncomfortable.

Receiving this gift was making him unable to speak. We gave him the guitar and forgot about it.

Three years passed. Then one day Sarah sent me a video of a teenager ripping up the electric guitar on stage, his hair whipping around, and the crowd loving his passion.

Yes, it was the teenager we had given a guitar to. Apparently, he took to it. He learned to play. He learned to perform. And he was fire itself on stage.

"I owe it all to you," he told me in an email.

Actually, he owed it all to the unexpected kindness of Dimitry, and the kindness of Sarah in arranging for us to meet. You never know what wonders may come from the unexpected kindness you do. Miracles await.

> *"One can pay back the loan of gold, but one lies forever in debt to those who are kind."*
>
> —MALAYSIAN PROVERB

Melissa Etheridge is a rock and roll god. I've been a fan for decades. The fact that I had a private songwriting lesson with her, in her home, with just her and me riffing, and me even singing for her (gasp) was miraculous. But I wasn't going to mention it as an act of unexpected kindness, as I paid to be there. She was fulfilling a transaction. But when I saw her again, she did something she didn't have to do.

After my private session with her, I flew back home to Texas and went to work. I was inspired. I wrote new songs. I named my album, "The Great Something," changing it from "Miracle" after a conversation with Melissa. I also wrote a song just for Melissa. I was proud of the album. I gathered my Band of Legends, and we recorded it. When it was complete, I sent CDs to Melissa, but I never heard back.

Then she was performing in San Antonio. I bought front row tickets, of course. But I also searched for a way to reconnect with the rock legend. I knew her bass player was best friends with my drummer. So I asked my guy to contact her guy and see if there was a way for me to connect with Melissa before or after her show.

There was.

I met her after the show, standing by her tour bus, getting dizzy smelling the exhaust fumes as I waited for her to meet her fans. When she saw me, she smiled big. She knew I was there. She had seen me during the show and blew a kiss at me from stage. And when she and her band were exiting after their final number, she turned around and said—in front of thousands of people—"I love you, Joe."

By the tour bus, I waited. She saw me, walked right up to me, and hugged me long and hard. After introducing her to my wife at the time and two of our friends, I asked the question that was keeping me up.

"Did you get my new album?"

"Yes, I did! Thank you!"

"What did you think of it?"

I held my breath.

This was the moment of no return. If she didn't like it, I'm sunk. If she did like it, I might ride the kind words forever. Mark Twain said he could live two weeks on a good compliment. One from Melissa would take me to my grave.

Melissa slowly turned and looked at the handful of people around her. I assumed later that she was checking to see if anyone was filming her. No one was. She turned to me and said the words that made my knees buckle.

"I loved it," she said. "It is great."

I stared and then folded. I could no longer look her in the eye. Being a fan, hearing these enormous words, were almost too much. I felt I might faint.

"Keep playing, singing, and writing," she said. "You'll only get better and better."

I only know what she said today because my friends heard the words and repeated them to me after the moment. I was about to faint.

"Look me up next time," Melissa said. "Let's get together."

Melissa Etheridge's act of unexpected kindness is still with me. I dedicated my album to her. So far it's been the last one I've recorded, mostly due to my life being swept up with divorce, deaths of family members, a new relationship, and a pandemic. But the seed has been planted. And one day new music will be born.

All thanks to Melissa Etheridge.

> *"The smallest act of kindness is worth*
> *more than the greatest intention."*
> —KAHLIL GIBRAN

It's embarrassing to admit just how terrified I was, but I didn't want to perform on stage as a singer-songwriter, fronting my own band, even though I had agreed to do so.

I had nightmares about it.

I had day tremors about it.

I wanted to back out of it.

Though I was sixty-five years old at the time (and working on year seventy as I write this) and had been on stages around the world as a speaker, being on stage as a singer was completely different.

Actor Kevin Bacon is a musician, too. He said acting was easy compared to performing on stage. He admitted it scared him shitless.

So why did I agree to perform in the first place?

Meghan.

Meghan Cathlin Sandau heard me speak at a luncheon that I spoke at as a favor to a friend. I wasn't paid. I didn't get to sell books. I spoke for free and was given a hamburger to eat.

Some deal, right?

But you never know who is in the audience. There were only sixteen people, but one changed my life forever.

"I used to promote big concerts," Meghan told me. "If you ever want help with your music, I'm your girl."

It's easy to blurt out things in the moment, when there's no reality to wake you up to what you are saying.

"I've wanted to perform with my band," I said. "They are all pros. They've helped me record six singer-songwriter albums. They are urging me to perform with them."

"Do you want a big event or a small one?"

Big event?

"I can have you open for Madonna." I internally gasped for air.

Madonna?

"Or Huey Lewis and the News."

My mouth was letting flies in.

"How big do you want to go?" she asked.

Can't I start with a front porch someplace? I thought.

"We can do a nightclub or outdoor arena or whatever you want," she said. "Big one or small one."

Small one? I thought to myself.

Exactly.

Meghan and I stayed in touch via email and text and a coffee date or two. Her husband at the time was an investor in a small night club in downtown Austin. They had a stage and held informal concerts. She offered to show it to me. I agreed.

I got my muses together. Sarah McSweeney, Lori Anderson, Meghan, and I all went to see The Townsend. We loved the location, look, and feel. The concert area held about fifty people tops. I thought it would be ideal for my first show.

I walked around the little room. I stood on the little stage and pretended I was getting a standing ovation. I was programming my mind for success. I had the ladies take photos of me. I had photos with each of them. The more I stayed in the room, the more I felt comfortable in it.

"Let's do it," I told the ladies.

We set a date for three months out.

My intention had been declared.

I went back home and felt the fears of a lifetime crawl up my back and eat at my brain.

My band was ready. They weren't nervous. Performing is like breathing to them. I call them The Band of Legends for a reason.

But me, I wanted out.

Sarah met with me a few times to calm my nerves and coach me in performing.

"If there were a way to get out of this," I told her. "I'd take it. But I teach to face your fears and I need to face mine."

It felt like my fears were winning.

I had lunch with Jen Sincero, author of *You Are a Badass*. I loved her book, promoted it, and knew she had been in a band. I told her my fears. She just stared. I don't think she believed me, but my terrors were real.

I practiced daily. I picked the handful of songs I wanted to perform.

Meghan was there every step of the way. She heard my fears. She listened. She urged me to process my feelings and fears.

At one point I created an alternative personality that I could pretend was me. I loved creating a character and a story around Antonio Bembe. Just thinking about him made me feel stronger. I shared the writing with Meghan. She loved it. She would call me Antonio in our emails.

Meghan even sent out news releases to the media promoting the 2017 event. One read:

As seen in Rolling Stone magazine, Dr. Joe delivers "self-help rock" in original tunes full of wisdom and passion. He's been compared to Leonard Cohen and Tom Petty, but remains a one-of-a-kind ball of fire. His new album, "The Great Something," is dedicated to the rock icon Dr. Joe studied songwriting with, Melissa Etheridge. His "Band of Legends" include drummer Joe Vitale, bass man Glenn Fukunaga, and lead guitarist Daniel Barrett.

My terror remained.

Desperate, I signed up for an online Masterclass on performance, taught by Usher. I had no idea who he was. I just knew it was on performing. It turned out to be a magnificent in-depth course. He covered virtually everything about performing. But Usher said one thing that truly helped.

"You'll rehearse and do everything to make your show great," I think he said. "But on the night of the show, something will go wrong."

He went on to explain that knowing something will go wrong made it easier to handle when and if something, in fact, did go wrong. Years later I would learn it is a technique from ancient Stoicism: practice the inevitable challenge.

The night came and my band and I performed. Meghan was there. She had created little things with big impact. She took a photo of me hugging Melissa Etheridge and put it on stage, facing me. Only I could see it. It was empowering.

And yes, something did go wrong. Lightning blew out power. Friends didn't make it; they were stuck in traffic. I didn't have my songs memorized and needed to use music stands.

The show was easy, all things considered, and my band and I received a standing ovation. But if it hadn't been for the unexpected kindness of Meghan, my musical dreams would have remained only a dream.

> *"You can accomplish by kindness*
> *what you cannot by force."*
> —PUBLILIUS SYRUS

When I landed in Bangkok, I was tired, frustrated, and apprehensive. I didn't want to go. The long flights and crowded plane on the second leg of the journey made me weary. I didn't know the gentleman who paid to bring me there. I wasn't a fan of speaking, let alone long-distance international travel. But here I was in Bangkok.

Once I got through customs and made my way to the visitors greeting area, a young man with a GQ suit and a respectful smile came up to me. It was Andres Pira.

"Dr. Joe, welcome to Thailand." I instantly liked this young man, who hugged me and thanked me for the journey. He took my bags and led me to his van. There he told me a story I've never yet forgotten.

"I had been homeless here fifteen years ago," he explained. He's thirty-five now. He was twenty then. "My grandfather died and left me a little money. I blew it by leaving Sweden and going to the first warm climate I could get to."

Born and raised in Sweden, he hated the cold and long periods of darkness. He demonstrated his dislike with disobedience, even being in street gangs. When he could leave, he ran. But Thailand was no picnic. He didn't speak the language. He didn't know their customs. And his funds were limited. Before long, he was sleeping on the beaches of Phuket. Homeless.

"I called a friend of mine back home in Sweden but he wouldn't help me," Andres said. "He sent me a book. I was upset. I was starving. I didn't want a book. I wanted money."

The book was *The Secret*. Andres started reading it and scoffed.

"I'm going to prove this book wrong," he declared. "I'll prove this mumbo jumbo doesn't work."

He thought he would try something small, so he wished for a cup of coffee.

Someone bought him one.

"I thought that was a fluke, so I tried for lunch. But someone bought me lunch."

Andres kept increasing his goals until now, fifteen years later, he sat beside me in his van, a billionaire.

I was impressed. Thirty-five years old and a billionaire. All from applying what he learned from *The Secret*.

"Not just *The Secret*," he explained. "I read your books. Jack Canfield, Bob Proctor. I read the older works of Napoleon Hill, Charles Haanel, and Wallace Wattles. I kept studying and I kept applying."

Today he owns one of the largest real estate empires in Thailand. He also has twenty other businesses, from coffee shops and petrol stations to a gym.

"I owe it all to you," he said.

"You owe it all to yourself," I corrected. "I wrote the material. You applied it."

He brought me to Thailand for his first ever success event. He didn't plan to speak on stage, but after I heard his story, I told him he had to. I had to pep talk him into agreeing, but agree he did, and speak he did. His story inspired everyone.

But Andres had an additional gift for me. He arranged for me to spend a week in a resort in Phuket. The place was on the water, was quiet and serene, and held twelve people. But only I was there. Andres rented the place for me as a gift.

One night I sat on the side of the rail over the water, having a cigar and sipping a Scotch. I had this profound feeling that this was a gift from the universe, through Andres, to thank me for all who I had helped. I remember feeling the words from the silence, "This is your gift. Relax. Enjoy."

Andres and I became friends. Despite our wide age difference, I felt like he was my brother. We kidded each other. We spoke easily. We listened. I suggested he write a book and offered to help. His ended up being the biggest book deal of my career so far. The book became *Homeless to Billionaire*. Andres went on and the following year held another event, this time with Mike Tyson, Jack Canfield, and me as the main draws.

During my visits to Thailand, I learned the country was a gift-giving culture. On birthdays, people didn't expect gifts; they gave them. That was a shock to me.

Having been born near Christmas, I always complained that people gave me one gift and declared it was for both events. I always felt gypped. But Thailand awakened a new me. I quit looking for gifts and started giving them.

All of this, thanks to the unexpected kindness of Andres Pira.

> *"Kindness is the light that dissolves all walls between souls, families, and nations."*
> —PARAMAHANSA YOGANANDA

It seems harder to describe this next act of kindness because it's ongoing and ambiguous. I'm not sure who to give credit to. I'm referring to "The Great Something." What you might call God.

I wrote a song declaring that this "great something" has always been with me. Certainly, there were times when I didn't see it or feel it or realize it and would even deny it. But, in retrospect, I was always taken care of. There were also times of spectacular miracles.

Here's one of them.

When I was in college at Kent State University in the 1970s, I spent most of my time chasing books. Because I was a fan of the author Jack London, I wanted to read his semi-autobiographical novel, *Martin Eden*.

I walked to a used bookstore outside of downtown Kent. It was a cool place. It had been a bar in the early 1900s, maybe earlier, and still had the heavy wood bar, only then covered with books.

"Do you have *Martin Eden*?" I asked the owner, who by then knew me as a regular browser if not buyer at her rustic old store.

"I'm sure I do," and she led me to the fiction section. We both scoured the titles but couldn't find it.

"I guess we sold it," she said.

As I turned to leave the store, the entire room turned into a blur. It was as though everything blacked out. All the books were unreadable. But one book seemed to have a spotlight on it. There wasn't a light in the room. There were no floodlights or spotlights. Yet one book seemed to be highlighted with a golden hue. I beelined to it.

It was *Martin Eden*.

I grabbed it, showed the equally stunned owner, and bought it. I devoured it. I was in awe of the story, writing style, and ending. London's character commits suicide at the end. It was such a moving passage; I remember reading it to my brothers when I visited home. They were uncharacteristically polite. They listened. I don't remember if they got it. But I did. The book became an inspiration, which led me to fulfilling my calling to be an author.

But what put a light on that book? How did I find it, out of order from all books, not in the right section, and in such a way that it felt supernatural?

The Great Something led me to it.

I started to write a book called *The Great Something*, but never got past the first few pages. It may never become its own book. But I must acknowledge the kindness the creator has given to me. I've always felt protected, even in the worst of times. But protected by what?

The Great Something.

In case you are curious, here are the lyrics to my song *The Great Something*:

Angry at God, blood in my eyes,
Burning within, I felt no love inside
Life seemed unfair, all struggle and fight,
Nothing went my way, I felt lost with no light

I was homeless and mad
Even my soul felt despair
But thru it all I learned
Something greater cared

    Look for the signs of love
    Look for the signs of hope
    Look for the Great Something inside
    Look for the Great Something inside

I awakened with a shock,
To the Great Something inside,
Taking care of me no matter what,
Nudging me like a hidden ally

Thru the dark nights, and sad days
Thru the worries, and fears,
Thru the aches, and the tears,
It was guiding my way

Look for the signs of love
Look for the signs of hope
Look for the Great Something inside
Look for the Great Something inside

I almost died by my own hand
Almost begged for the shift
But I awakened to the plan
That everything was a gift

Life squeezes the good out of you
Forces you to reach beyond your stretch,
Urges you to live with no regrets,
Makes you grow and renew

Look for the signs of love
Look for the signs of hope
Look for the Great Something inside
Look for the Great Something inside

The teachers say
Be not afraid
You're safe always
Be not afraid
The Great Something says
Be not afraid
Be not afraid
Be not afraid

Look for the signs of love
Look for the signs of hope
Look for the Great Something inside
Look for the Great Something inside

> *"Be kind whenever possible. It is always possible."*
>
> —THE 14TH DALAI LAMA

Acts of unexpected kindness continue to happen in my life.

As I mentioned in the beginning of this little book, I wanted to focus on the gifts that came before I reached any level of global notoriety. Once people saw me as important or influential, they went out of their way to be kind. While I appreciate all of it, I wouldn't say much of it was unexpected. There was often an agenda to the kindness, an expectation of return.

I wanted to write this book more from the perspective of how people were kind to me when there was no clear pay off for them. They helped because it was altruistic; what they got was the good feeling of knowing they helped. Nothing more.

There's a show I've seen on Netflix called "The Kindness Diaries." The star of it, Leon Logothetis, travels the world, only eating, sleeping, or traveling further when someone has been kind to him. Complete strangers help him. They offer food, a place to stay, or fuel.

What none of these people know is that he is independently wealthy and looking for select people to give a leg up. I remember one episode where he saw a woman busking: singing on the streets for donations. He is moved to tears by her music and her story. She is open and unexpectedly kind. He then tells her he is going to pay for her education for the next year. Everyone cried, including me.

There are kind people doing loving things today, in my life and in the lives of others, including yours. What I challenge you to do is be a source of unexpected kindness to others. As these stories from my life demonstrate, sometimes little things make profound and lasting differences.

Your turn.

Go do an unexpected act of kindness.

How about one a day for the rest of your life?

How about doing one right now?

Expect Miracles.

Books of Unexpected Kindness

*B*ooks have been sources of unexpected kindness to me. Throughout *my life a special few have been my friends, allies, oracles, therapists, and more. I offer here some of my favorites, from a lifetime of reading. This is not a complete list, and in no particular order, just ones I remember and often reread.*

Man's Search for Meaning by Victor Frankl. A masterpiece. A classic. The author was a therapist who became a Nazi concentration camp prisoner. What Frankl learned about survival will change your life forever. Life has meaning, but you must search for the meaning. Read it.

Psycho-Cybernetics by Maxwell Maltz. If you only read one book from this list, this 1960 gem would be it. Maltz was a plastic surgeon who discovered real change happens inside, not outside.

Moonshots by Naveen Jain. Think the world is void of opportunities? Think again. Jain is mining for minerals on the moon and working to make illness optional. There are no limitations in the real world of abundance. An exhilarating manifesto.

Principles by Ray Dalio. Wisdom from the life experience of a billionaire. Not something you'll read in one day, but something you'll eat every day for a year. This is an operating manual for life and business. Detailed. Overwhelming. Mind boggling.

How to Win Friends and Influence People by Dale Carnegie. After reading a biography of Carnegie (*Self-Help Messiah*), I decided to read his famous book again. It is a *masterpiece*. I am *in awe* of Carnegie's conversational writing style, powerful stories, and crisp message. Priceless.

The Power of Impossible Thinking by Yoram and Cook. Life changing. It helps you think about your thinking, which frees you to think differently than your standard predictable patterns. I've put this title on every book list I've ever created. Read it.

The Book of est by Luke Rhinehart. Hypnotic. Loved it so much I published it after it went out of print. It's a fictional account of the infamous confrontational self-help seminar of the 1970s. Written so well you feel you are in the room. All about self-empowerment and personal responsibility. It'll make you squirm. I later met and interviewed the author, who also wrote The Dice Man, another book that influenced me when I was in high school.

Total Recall by Arnold Schwarzenegger. Incredibly terrific. Even "Fantastic!" I hyperventilated reading this autobiography by the bodybuilder, movie star, governor, and more. He learned his hardcore rules for success in the gym and applies them to everything. Exciting.

I, Mammal by Loretta Breuning. Enlightening. Read *all* of her books. She basically points out that you are a monkey with a reactionary monkey brain. As soon as you realize it, and with awareness and discipline, you can become less a monkey and more an awakened ape.

You Are the Placebo by Joe Dispenza. The author explains how it is possible to heal many "incurables" with thought alone, by detailing how the mind influences *everything*. In a way, this is a manual on how to create the placebo effect *as needed*. Fascinating.

The Elements of Eloquence by Mark Forsyth. Fun, funny, flippant. It will spin your writing into a spell generator. ("Spell" as in "I'll put a spell on you!") This charming book demonstrates the elements of eloquence while explaining them.

The Magic Power of Emotional Appeal by Roy Garn. I love this book so much I buy every edition I find and have read it a dozen times. Garn reveals that we are all emotionally led by the nose and shows how to use that fact to influence others. A gem.

The Third Door by Alex Banayan. When you want to achieve a goal, most people make a straight line to the front door. They do what everyone else does. Others join the inner circles of the influencers who might help them get what they want. But what if the front door is locked and the inner circle is barred? You look for (or create) "The Third Door." Anything *is* possible, but you may have to open the third door. Terrific book.

The Law of Success by Napoleon Hill. Get the 1928 (not 1925) version of this massive work by the famous *Think and Grow Rich* author. (Read *Think and Grow Rich*, too.) This giant volume was his magnum opus. Everything you need to know about success is here. Devour it.

Outwitting the Devil by Napoleon Hill. OMG. It was too hot to be published during Hill's lifetime and wasn't released until decades after his death. While fiction, the book made me sweat as I realized the "devil" was my own mind.

The Science of Storytelling by Will Storr. Let me tell you a story . . . You buy, sell, and share with stories. The better the story, the better the result. This brilliant book opened my eyes to how our minds work, so we can better communicate in a way that gets the results we want. Loved it.

Ego Is the Enemy by Ryan Holliday. I hate the title. But I'm sure that's my ego objecting to it. Holliday has single-handedly brought Stoicism to the masses. All of his books are brilliant, including *The Obstacle Is the Way* and *Stillness Is the Key*.

The Will to Live by Dr. Arnold A. Hutschnecker. This 1951 masterpiece reveals that your unconscious mind is running the show. You may not achieve what you want due to subconscious influences. This riveting book demonstrates how the inner mind works and helps guide you to clearing the hidden blocks to freedom.

The Robert Collier Letter Book by Robert Collier. Hands down the single most powerful book on copywriting. The metaphysical author was a legendary copywriter. His samples may seem dated but I've modeled many of my most successful letters on his work. Pure gold.

The Nature of Personal Reality by Jane Roberts. This is the "channeled" book that started it all. It's big and detailed and was the first to introduce me to beliefs and how they create reality. The ghostly "Seth" may or may not be the source, but the wisdom is practical and head spinning.

Rejection Proof by Jia Jiang. I stopped worrying about being rejected after reading this book. Great stories. Great fun.

The Science of Getting Rich by Wallace Wattles. Old (1910) but relevant. It inspired the movie *The Secret*, but it's more practical than woo-woo. Read it with focus to understand it.

Meditations. Hard to believe emperor Marcus Aurelius wrote this *to himself* two thousand years ago. He's the poster boy for Stoicism. It's the secret companion of truly great people. Deep.

The Courage to Be Disliked by Ichiro Kishimi and Fumitake Koga. A runaway bestseller in Asia. About understanding that you are a meaning creating machine. Change the meaning, change your life. Be ready to be fully you.

Sanity, Insanity, and Common Sense, a 1987 book by Rick Suarez, Roger Mills, and Darlene Stewart. A few gems from the book reveal its depth: "The fact is that in separate realities, everyone is right and everyone is telling the truth as they see it." "Stress is a byproduct of thinking; it is not inherent in situations or circumstances." "A reality is an *apparency*. It is how something *appears* to be." Whew. Wisdom.

Pollyanna by Eleanor Porter. This 1913 classic is delightfully written with all the energy of an action movie, and at the same time brilliantly conveys one of the simplest and most profound self-help methods of all time. Read it and learn how to play The Glad Game, too. Gold.

The Power of Neuroplasticity by Shad Helmstetter. Conversational guide on how to scientifically use your brain to achieve goals. Based on solid research. Genius.

The Practical Visionary by Corinne McLaughlin. Offers overwhelming proof that every social problem you can name is being addressed. While the mainstream media rarely nods in the direction of the good deeds people are doing, seeing all this evidence for the positive is wonderful. Shows you how to be a practical visionary, too. Inspiring. Refreshing.

The Yamas & Niyamas by Deborah Adele. A spiritual masterpiece. Explores how to use the ten ethical guidelines of yoga practice to have a meaningful life. Beautifully written with examples that bring the tenets to life.

Stratagems by Frontinus. Written in the first century AD by a general from ancient Rome, this fascinating collection of true stories reveals creative military strategies from Greek and Roman history. Very readable, surprising, and entertaining.

Personality Isn't Permanent by Benjamin Hardy, Ph.D. Empowering. Liberating. The idea of making choices now that my "Future Self" will thank me for later is enough to recommend this great book, but there's far more juice in it, all about breaking free of mental limits. Read it.

Martin Eden by Jack London. My eighteen-year-old mind was vividly influenced by this famous semi-autobiographical novel from 1909. It made me commit to being an author, no matter what. Fortunately, I didn't take my own life, as had Eden in the book, and London later in life.

The Magic of Believing by Claude Bristol. This 1948 self-help masterpiece influenced everyone from showman Liberace and comedian Phyllis Diller to me. I read it as a teenager and never forgot the feeling of empowerment it gave me then, and still does today. A beloved classic.

Zen in the Art of Writing by Ray Bradbury. Originally published in 1973 as a slim chapbook but thickened with new essays and republished multiple times since, I found this famous sci-fi author's gusto for writing to be exhilarating.

Fortunes For All by Vash Young. Young's 1931 book, *A Fortune to Share*, shook my world when I first read it around 2018, as it probably did all readers of it during the Great Depression. It gave hope. It became a national bestseller. Vash wrote several follow-up books. But his final one is my favorite. Published in 1959, when Young was past seventy years old, it details a life of gratitude and giving. Your fortune is in your mind and how you use it. I adore this book.

Consciously Creating Circumstances by George Winslow Plummer. I've not stop rereading this little book from 1953, the year I was born, though I probably didn't stumble across it until the 1980s. I love its clear articulation of complex spiritual ideas. It explains mind power, how to create thought forms, and how they go into the world to create what you want. The author's book was unexpected kindness.

Letters From a Stoic by Seneca. His letters from two hundred centuries ago speak to me today, as if he wrote them to me personally. It was unexpectedly kind of Seneca to purposely think of future generations, and pass along his hard-earned wisdom to us.

At Your Command by Neville. Neville Goddard's first book was so influential to me, I republished it decades after he died. He wrote and spoke about "feeling it real;" imagining that what you want is already yours. I love all his books. I wish I could have met him.

Joe Vitale Bibliography

This is a partial list of published books and does not include coauthored books, online courses, digital products, podcasts, apps, or movies.

Books

1. *The Abundance Paradigm* (2022)
2. *Adventures Within* (2003)
3. *Karmic Marketing* (2021)
4. *The Fifth Phrase* (2021)
5. *Hypnotic Selling Secrets* (2022)
6. *The Secret to Attracting Money* (2021)
7. *Money Loves Speed: From Stress to Success: Revealing the 8 Laws* (2020)
8. *The Art & Science of Results* (2020)
9. *Anything Is Possible: 7 Steps for Doing the Impossible* (2018)
10. *Greatest Law of Attraction Quotes* (2017)

11. Hypnotic Marketing (2005 and 2015)
12. AT Zero (2013)
13. *Faith* (2013)
14. *The Abundance Manifesto* (2013)
15. *Healing Music* (2013)
16. *Attract Money Now* (2012)
17. *The Awakening Course* (2011)
18. *The Attractor Factor* (2005 and 2009)
19. *The Secret Prayer* (2009)
20. *The Miracle: Six Steps to Enlightenment* (2016)
21. *There's a Customer Born Every Minute: P.T. Barnum's Amazing 10 "Rings of Power" for Creating Fame, Fortune, and a Business Empire Today* (1998 and 2006)
22. *Zero Limits* (2007)
23. *Hypnotic Writing* (1995 and 2006)
24. *The Key* (2007)
25. *Life's Missing Instruction Manual* (2007)
26. *Expect Miracles: The Missing Secret* (2008)
27. *Buying Trances* (2007)
28. *The Seven Lost Secrets of Success* (1992 and 2007)
29. *Instant Manifestation* (2011)
30. *The Awakened Millionaire* (2016)
31. *The Miracles Manual: The Secret Coaching Sessions* (2013) (Three volumes)
32. *The Greatest Money-Making Secret in History* (2003)
33. *Spiritual Marketing* (2001) (Retitled *The Attractor Factor*)
34. *CyberWriting* (1996)
35. *The AMA Complete Guide to Small Business Advertising* (1994)
36. *Zen and the Art of Writing* (1984)

Spoken Audio Programs

The Awakening Course

The Missing Secret

The Secret to Attracting Money

The Abundance Paradigm

The Ultimate Law of Attraction Library

The Zero Point

The Power of Outrageous Marketing

Singer-songwriter Albums (with the Band of Legends)

One More Day

Strut!

Sun Will Rise

The Healing Song

Reflection

The Great Something

Alternative Music Albums

Blue Healer

Afflatus

Stretch (with Ruthie Foster and Daniel Barrett)

No Words (with the Band of Legends)

Instrumental Albums (with Guitar Monk Mathew Dixon)

At Zero

Aligning to Zero

432 to Zero

Invoking Divinity

Higher Octaves

The Enlightenment Audio

About the Author

Dr. Joe Vitale—once homeless but now a motivating inspirator known to his millions of fans as "Mr. Fire!"—is the world-renowned author of numerous bestselling books, such as *The Attractor Factor*, *Zero Limits*, *Life's Missing Instruction Manual*, *The Secret Prayer*, *Attract Money Now* (free at www.AttractMoneyNow.com), *The Awakened Millionaire*, *Karmic Marketing*, *Hypnotic Writing*, and *The Miracle*, to name a few.

A media personality seen on TV shows around the world, his weekly online television program "Zero Limits Living" can be watched at www.ZeroLimitsLivingTV.com as well as on 1,000 platforms around the world, and his podcast can be heard at www.JoeVitalePodcast.com.

He is considered one of the top fifty most inspiring speakers in the world. He travels around the globe, sharing his uplifting messages, and inspiring stories on stages everywhere.

He starred in the blockbuster movie *The Secret*, as well as a dozen other films. His own movie, *Zero Limits*, will be released in 2023.

He has recorded many bestselling audio programs, from *The Missing Secret* to *The Zero Point*.

He's also the world's first self-help singer-songwriter, with sixteen albums out and many of his songs nominated for the Posi Award (considered the Grammys of positive music). His latest album, called *The Great Something*, was inspired by and dedicated to legendary performer Melissa Etheridge.

Dr. Joe Vitale created Miracles Coaching®, The Awakening Course, The Secret Mirror, Hypnotic Writing, Advanced Ho'oponopono Certification, Zero Limits Mastery, Miracles Mastermind, and many more life transforming courses and products.

He lives outside of Austin, Texas with his love, bestselling author, artist, vocalist, and media darling Lisa Winston.

Follow Dr. Joe Vitale via:

TikTok: DrJoeVitale
Instagram: DrJoeVitale
TV Show: www.ZeroLimitsLivingTV.com
Podcast: www.JoeVitalePodcast.com
Coaching: www.MiraclesCoaching.com
Twitter: https://twitter.com/mrfire
Blog: http://blog.mrfire.com/
Facebook: https://www.facebook.com/drjoevitale
YouTube: https://www.youtube.com/user/JoeMrFire
Main website: www.MrFire.com